# Social Intelligence for the Socially Awkward

A Practical How-To Guide for Speed-Reading People and Social Dynamics, Having Magnetic Charisma, and Dominating Social Circles

## GERALD CONFIENZA

© 2018 GERALD CONFIENZA. All rights reserved.

The contents of this book may not be reproduced, duplicated or transmitted without direct written permission from the author.

**Legal Notice:**
You cannot amend, distribute, sell, use, quote or paraphrase any part of the content of this book without the consent of the author.

**Disclaimer Notice:**
Please note the information contained in this document is for educational and entertainment purposes only. No warranties of any kind are expressed or implied. Readers acknowledge that the author is not engaging in the rendering of legal, financial, medical or professional advice.
By reading this document, the reader agrees that under no circumstances is the author responsible for any losses, direct or indirect, which are incurred as a result of the use of the information contained within this document, including, but not limited to, errors, omissions, or inaccuracies.

# Table of Contents

Social Intelligence: ...................................................................................... 7

A Brief Introduction ..................................................................................... 7

Chapter 1: How Socially Awkward Are You and Why That Is So ..................... 10

Chapter 2: Mindset Shift: Limiting Beliefs About Yourself Means Limiting Your Reality ........................................................................................................ 14

Chapter 3: Body Language Secrets ............................................................... 22

Chapter 4: Tonality ...................................................................................... 33

Chapter 5: Conversations ............................................................................. 52

Chapter 6: Social Momentum and Calibration ............................................... 79

Chapter 7: Networking in Work Environments .............................................. 88

Chapter 8: Dating Perfection: How to Impress the Opposite Sex Without Looking like a Dunce ................................................................................... 94

Chapter 9: Social Media Leverage for Social Intelligence ............................. 102

One Small Favor ........................................................................................ 109

Conclusion ................................................................................................ 110

A Preview of…Find Your Passion: The Ultimate No BS Workbook ................ 112

A Gift for You ............................................................................................ 129

Bibliography .............................................................................................. 131

# Social Intelligence:
# A Brief Introduction

There's so much talk about IQ nowadays; people boasting about their IQ scores and how smart they really are. Poor wimps, only if they would understand that IQ in social circles is as important as sprinkles on ice cream; you like them, but they are of no use if you don't have a scoop of ice cream in the first place.

Now you might ask: "So, then, what is that scoop of ice cream and how can I get it?" This question is extremely important to all of us as:

a) Everybody loves ice cream.
b) This entire book centers upon your aim to get it for yourself and my advice to make it happen for you.

Now to the answer: the scoop of ice cream is Social Intelligence. Your IQ matters a lot, but it's of no use if you can't back it up with a great sense of Social Intelligence. For many of you, this might be a new term. But this is extremely relevant, and I cannot stress just how important it really is for your success in any social relationship or circle.

Social Intelligence simply refers to the art of socialization. It can be considered as your ability to interact with the people around you and form long-lasting and healthy relationships with them.

There is another difference between Social Intelligence and IQ (or Intelligence Quotient), and that is the fact that Social Intelligence can be acquired but IQ is something that you're born with. So, you can blame your parents for not giving you the required genes for a higher IQ, but Social Intelligence is something that can be worked upon, acquired and expanded. It is due to this very reason that despite not being the smartest one out there, you have the ability to have a great social life with this simple yet effective tool that we'll be focusing on: Social Intelligence.

Haven't you wondered how some people just have it so easy? I mean, just look at them! No matter where they go, they are the attraction of each party, group, couple or relationship. Hell, you could be a rocket scientist sitting at a meeting in NASA and that guy shows up with a high-school degree (possibly even a drop out) and he'll have the audacity to come and talk like he knows where you'll find the hidden city of gold on Mars! And the magic in all of this lies in the fact that everyone will believe him because he is that damn good at orating and presenting his ideas and logic.

Why? What has he actually done here? What's the trick or mantra that he is following? Now listen closely to this line, right here, as this is where your life changes for the better. I'm introducing you to the power to change how people look at you in society. In this book, I'm going to teach you how to reincarnate yourself into what you want to be and not what people think you are. You will be given the power to reinvent a character like the writer of a play, because you, my dear friend, are the writer of your life; a life that is a theatrical performance in itself. And it is your own responsibility to make it worthwhile.

This book shall teach you how to become a social king and crack the code to Social Intelligence. Once you're done with this book, you'll know what to say, how to say it, when to say it, whom to say it to- the whole nine yards. You'll have the spotlight effect in life!

As I said, your life is like a theatrical performance. You are the writer, the director, the actor, the backstage crew, the props; everything and everyone on stage! The only thing that you're not is the audience and at the end of the day, they are the ones that truly matter for the success of your performance. But guess what? You have the power to influence them and show them how great a show you can put up. No matter how many faults your performance has and how many times you forget your lines and actions, what matters is what the audience sees.

If you have the ability to conceal all the flaws in your performance, then it's as good as a flawless one! Social kings are people who make mistakes during their performance, as everyone does, but the audience never gets to know, and that is the secret behind their success.

So, join me as I take you on a journey to conquer your own life and move on to inspire others. Go and look at the mirror today and wave your old self-goodbye. Get ready for a new and successful social life through your domination in each social circle that you step into. Allow me to introduce you to this step by step guide to achieve Social Intelligence which will surely change your life for the better!

# Chapter 1

# How Socially Awkward Are You and Why That Is So

Being socially awkward is not a crime and you shouldn't be ashamed of accepting that you are the way you are. But it is also true that everything in life is directly or indirectly related to the choices that you make. If you do face social anxiety, you made a great choice by starting this book. Congratulations on that! Always remember that the only two things that you have no control over are your birth and your death. Social anxiety is something that can be cured and you are on the right track to beat it!

**A test for social anxiety and awkwardness:**

The following test will give you a numerical representation as to how affected you might be with social anxiety. Now remember; this is not being conducted by a psychologist or psychiatrist, so variations are bound to happen. To minimize these deviations, I would advise you to answer each question honestly. Remember that no one is looking at you or judging you. Your first step to ridding yourself of this problem is to diagnose it and this test will help you do so.

Given below are random statements which describe situations that you might face in real life. Assess them, absorb their scenario and imagine yourself to be in them. Then rate your anxiety on a scale of 0 to 3 if you were to face each of those situations. To make your final score easier to calculate, I suggest that you find a page and start jotting down the individual score of each answer so you can add those all up once you're done.

After the test, I have listed a few general category observations for you to assess your score with. Do not read those remarks before taking the test as studies have proven that psychological tests lose their effectiveness once the subjects are told the expected outcomes of the study. Trick your mind into believing that there is no test and you'll be able to reach the most accurate score possible.

Remember: if you fake this test, you might end up having five minutes of forged satisfaction on your not facing social anxiety. But finding out that you have a problem and curing it is a far better option than telling yourself that you don't face an issue and living with it for the rest of your life.

Here are the statements for your test:

1. Giving a brief talk in front of six people.
2. Having a general conversation with someone who cares about you.
3. Saying hello to a stranger and indulging in a small discussion.
4. Talking to other students/colleagues in your class/workplace.
5. Answering your phone without looking at who's calling.
6. Driving with 3 other people in the car with you.
7. Telling your neighbors that their party was too loud last night and you'd like them to be quieter.
8. Asking a salesperson for help at any store.
9. Singing at a karaoke bar while sober.
10. Giving a presentation to your work team or at school.

Now here are the general categories for your score.

- **A score between 0-7:**

Chances are that you are not socially anxious and are probably having a good time with the people around you. If you are not, I suggest that you stick around because you'll find some great tips and techniques to make sure that your social life gleams in its perfection.

- **A score between 7-15:**

Adequate level of social anxiety can be found in your character. Nothing to worry about; just keep on reading and you'll cure this problem before you even know it.

- **A score between 15-30:**

You are highly socially anxious and often feel awkward while interacting with people. You also find it hard to socialize effectively. Chances are that you have faced great problems and hurdles in life due to this very reason. I advise you to read each chapter of this book closely and implement the techniques that are taught within them. As I said, nothing is impossible to beat and social anxiety is the same. At least you're on the right track to beat it!

**True self-acceptance:**

Before we move on to anything else, I want you to first accept your score. Now, that does not mean that you yield in front of the problem and accept it as a permanent disorder. I do not want you to believe the crap that you are who you are and that you can not change that. The world's worst advice is to accept who you are, regardless of how much you suck at something, and then putting in no effort whatsoever to rectify the issues that you are facing; all in the name of self-acceptance.

*Accepting that you have a problem while constantly striving towards its is true self-acceptance.* Learn this mantra by heart. The first step to curing or ridding yourself from a problem is to accept that it exists. You are done with that first step now and are on your way to cure your problem for good!

**"Okay, I accept that I have a problem. Now what?"**

Now this is where your journey begins. You have identified the problem and are looking for a solution. The best solution to your social awkwardness or anxiety is to address your problems one by one in a sequential yet complete manner. In this book, we are going to rectify your social life by working on your ability to make friends, to create a conversation and be able to hold it, to talk with conviction and impress people (yeah, that includes the opposite sex!).

I will teach you through a series of tried and tested steps that will ensure that you're a pro at speech and socialization. We will talk about tonality and the pitch of your voice, pauses, stress words and what not!

Your best shot at becoming a social king is to take into account all of the above traits that I have mentioned and work on them alongside this book. Read and understand what I'm providing you as an outtake and then start implementing it in your life; one point at a time. You will have to force it in the start, but soon you'll see how it all starts to gel in with who you are and before you know it, people will have forgotten your old fidgety self because they will be too busy admiring your new confident personality!

# Chapter 2

# Mindset Shift: Limiting Beliefs About Yourself Means Limiting Your Reality

**You are your own enemy:**

The human race has seen and narrated great epics in its sojourn on this planet. What constitutes these epics is undoubtedly a strong story, a protagonist and an antagonist, that is, a hero and a villain. As human beings, we are always reflecting upon stories and finding in them similarities to our own lives, sentiments and passions. That is how we relate to stuff that is being told to us; we like to feel that we're living our own little story.

The sad part of this is that we're always looking for the antagonist in our life, because duh! We aren't villains, right! We are the heroes of our story and it is our responsibility to find that character that's evil and wants to do something creepy to us so we can fight them. This outlook in life is extremely pointless and frankly stupid!

We are our own enemy before anyone else is. How is that? In any situation in life, before anyone else bars our way, our mind takes over and limits us by telling that we are not capable of doing what we have set out for. It tells us that, "Hey, it sounds like a pretty nice idea and all, but you know you're not *that* kinda' guy!" or "Yeah, you can sing. But you'll be shaking up on the stage." or "You could talk to that girl, but frankly she is way out of your league."

If you think that way, then you're definitely going to either not try at all, or fail even before you start because you're just expecting yourself to. The reason is that our beliefs impact our actions. No matter how hard we try, we can't change who we are until we refute our limiting beliefs about ourselves.

What we fail to realize about limiting beliefs is that because of them, our mind just ends the game without the referee even blowing the whistle to start it. We lose the match before it even begins and that's the saddest story that you could write for yourself.

You don't need to find a villain in your life. Forget them! Why? Because you should be too busy fighting your own self to stop it from destroying your life. Yes, someone might be plotting a master plan to fail you in whichever endeavor you are thinking to take. But you won't ever reach that state where they might put their plan into action until you actually undergo an action yourself and start doing something. If you give in to your mind and its limiting beliefs, then you are your biggest enemy.

Yes, if you start out positive, it doesn't mean that it's all going to pan out well for you. That's the difference between the fiction stories that we hear and the real life; there is no "happily ever after" in the latter. There are constant problems and hurdles and a lot of times, these hurdles bar us from reaching our destination. But it is better to lose midway than to never have the confidence to start working for what you want.

**Write down your problems and future goals:**

Today, on your first day of working on your social self, I want you to write down your negative and limiting beliefs about your character and set goals to refute those beliefs. Your first task is to alter your perception about yourself.

You must be wondering why I'm asking you to write them down when you know best about who you are and what are your beliefs about your own self.

Well, in 1992, a British psychologist conducted a study on hip and knee surgery patients. She gave a handout to all the patients which highlighted their weekly physiotherapy schedule. In the end of that handout, she provided 12 blank pages to them, one for each week of physiotherapy, to optionally write their weekly goals such as going for a random walk in the park.

She found that out of all the patients, the ones who wrote down their goals in the most detailed manner were able to recover the fastest from these surgeries and the intense and painful sessions of physiotherapy. They cured themselves at least two times faster than those who did not write down their goals and took physiotherapy without them!

Only if you write down your problems and goals, you will be surprised at learning new things about yourself. You will find views and points that you had never before thought of because you never looked at it the way you do as a writer.

The psychologist also found that the written word has a contract-binding feel to it. You are more likely to do something after you have written it down as compared to a situation where you merely agreed to do it. Our brain relates the written word with a holy aspect of being true and definite.

Using the same principal, I want you to write down the answer to some questions in a secret notebook and hide it away from everyone else. Just put it somewhere like a cupboard where you can review it later as we proceed. Try to be as detailed as possible while you answer the following questions.

- How do you look?
- How do you sound?
- What do others think of you?
- Would you like to be friends if you met your own self?
- How funny are you?
- How social are you?

Now that you have written down how you view yourself, I want you to review your answers as a third person. Then close the notebook and take five minutes alone to think about all that you have written. Can you identify your problems? If no, that is completely fine. To be honest with you, most people find it hard to pinpoint their own problems. These answers would still help you by the end of this book so I urge you to put pen on paper and write down the answers to these questions.

Even if you couldn't pinpoint your problems, you still do know where you want to be in the future. How you wish to sound, interact, socialize or give speeches. What is your goal by the time you are done with this book and have worked on yourself? Think about these goals and aims.

Then open that notebook again and write down your goals. They could be anything and everything from making new friends to singing at a concert. A random list of goals for anyone could look like this:

*"By the time I am done with this book, I will:*

- *Talk confidently in a group.*

- *Make new friends.*
- *Express myself fearlessly in front of new people.*
- *Go out to a restaurant all by my own.*
- *Take friends out on my own car."*

**Breaking negative beliefs and constructing positive ones:**

Understand that I am not providing you with a magical formula to set everything right. Your beliefs about yourself have been carved into place by years and years of your viewing yourself in a particular way. All of these problems will not just go away by writing them down. If you do not wish to be cured, then no one can help you. I often give this example that every student in a class is taught by the same teacher. But through that same teacher, some students are able to learn immensely and get amazing grades while others struggle with the subject.

The reason is that those students that secured a good grade were probably more receptive than those who thought they were putting in some good effort to pass the class but failed. Why did they fail when they got the same amount of time and attention from the same teacher? Yes, your intellect and ability to pick minute details of information do factor in to all of this, but on a general scale, the difference lies in the receptiveness of the students. If they are just sitting in class and thinking that this should be enough to make them pass the subject, then they are definitely on their way to fail.

Similarly, as your teacher for socialization, I am writing down detailed steps to help you learn this art of social intelligence. If you are just reading this book and thinking that it will magically make you a pro at socialization, then I'm sorry, but this won't work. First, you need to be receptive to all that I'm telling you through these words. You need to challenge yourself and your beliefs before anything else. You are not a coward or an awkward person. At this point in time, I want you to have a clean slate. I want your outlook about yourself to be rid of limitations and your mindset to be ready for change and action.

There is no end to who you are and what you can be. I want you to forget everything that has been told to you by your parents, your friends or your colleagues. Become a receptive soul that wishes to grow and overcome any obstacle that stands in its way.

Break your negative beliefs about yourself because they are nothing but a hurdle that stops you from achieving greatness. All the greats in history never made it by chance. Yes, many of them were extraordinary by birth, but they became the greatest only by rewiring their minds to believe that they could achieve anything! This was possible because all of them had two similar qualities:
- They never limited themselves to anything.
- They believed that everything was possible.

**Own your fluidity:**

This brings me to the second part of this therapy. Make positive beliefs about yourself; that you have what it takes to be funny, social, energetic and likeable. You are not a rigid character, but fluid in nature. You can alter yourself and change forms. It is possible for you to become anyone and anything because you hold no negative beliefs that limit you to be just one thing. You are going to work on becoming an intellectual that is also funny, on becoming someone who is outspoken but not rude, on being confident but not bitchy! You are not a color but a rainbow; you are not defined by a particular shade but constitute all colors within yourself.

**Being a free and undefined character:**

Although a 2013 study which was published in "Frontiers in Human Neuroscience" debunked the theory that humans only use 10% of their brain, but the fact remains that no one has ever been able to use all of their brain capacity. We have it in us to constantly and indefinitely grow and create new things.

Why not create a new character? Why not let the limiting beliefs stay behind while we take a stroll down the creation lane of our brains and brainstorm on why we need to be one thing at a time? Why can't we be everything all the time! Why can't we be the best thing for the best time!

It is human nature that we get bored after we have been conditioned to one thing for too long. Imagine that you're someone with such a swift and fluid character that you are everything that anyone could ever think of!

As I said, you are both the character and the writer of the play that you're presenting to the audience. Being the writer gives you the ability to write whatever you want your character to be. You will use your props and costume to create a guise that embodies each character for you.

The greatest actors are those that live their characters. Heath Ledger is famous for allegedly losing his mind after playing a stunner role as "The Joker" in the 2008 Batman film, "The Dark Knight." People praised him for it because he got so involved into the role that he never seemed to be able to get out of it.

I do not wish for you to limit yourself to being someone like Ledger because I believe that you have the ability to be even better than him!

Heath Ledger wasn't able to pull himself out of his character, but with the right amount of practice, you can!

I want you to be fluid enough to be able to change your role once it ends and you wish to slide into another one. I want you to believe that you are an actor capable of pulling off each role that is assigned to you. To teach you how to do that is my responsibility and believing that you can is yours.

This sensation that you'll undergo, of being everything in the world, is an addiction that you'll crave for in your life. Break those limiting beliefs so that you may give yourself away to this beautiful addiction and believe in nothing but the fact that you are fluid and will find your way around anything!

# Chapter 3

# Body Language Secrets

Body language is an integral part of your social life. Although we do not realize it ourselves, but the people around us can probably tell that we have a set pattern or way of expressing how we feel. Even without us opening our mouths, our family or significant other might ask why we look so down or what makes us so happy. This sounds extremely textbook, but to be really honest with you, it isn't!

Language is the primary but local form of expression. Body language, on the other hand, is universal for all primary emotions. No matter where you go in the world, the body language or facial expressions for happiness, sorrow, fear and sadness remain the same. Rest of all the feelings in life are a mixture and variation of these primary emotions and hence have no distinct expression across the globe. Such secondary emotions like love, excitement or being bored vary with culture and from person to person.

Controlling your body language means controlling how the world views you. There are always going to be moments in life when you have to undergo risky conversations. At that particular moment, the importance of body language amplifies manifold. Say you have to go and tell your boss that he is probably messing something up. Your body language along with the specific set of words that you'll use to convey your reservation for his decision or line of action are what would factor upon his perceiving that you're being disrespectful or actually looking out for him and the company. This situation has the potential of both you being stuck in the same post forever or you getting promoted instantly because your boss likes you.

Some people just feel so homely and easy to be with. You might have noticed that some of your friends just naturally feel easy to talk to. The reason is that their body language never makes you feel that they're being judgmental or getting tired of listening to your stuff. They seem welcoming and that's why you rank them above all other friends.

If you're a teen and you come home late, your mother might give you a long and stern look and that is enough to make you realize that you're in some trouble. Now what do you do in response to that? Either you scurry away from sight or make sure to check your actions and words in her presence; both a form of molding your body language according to the body language presented by your mother.

# 4 Types of body language that you use in daily life

Before we proceed on to reading other people's body language and modifying your own, we first need to understand the complete scope of body language itself. Once you see the complete picture of each type of basic body language, you might realize that you've been doing something wrong or ignoring a particular type that might help you instantly click at socialization.

**Facial expressions:**

The first and most obvious type of body language is facial expressions. Nature has not bestowed you with any primary structure that has no use in your life. Consider any body part that you primarily had at birth and you'll find a use for it. But eyebrows do nothing, right? I mean they are just sitting there and watching your life roll by.

Wrong! Your eyebrows serve a basic function to enhance facial expressions. Without eyebrows, your facial expressions would dim and might not be registered by the other person. This shows how important even nature perceives your facial expressions to be.

As mentioned above, the basic facial expressions for happiness, sorrow, fear and anger are the same throughout the world. Facial expressions for these as well as other emotions can help you express and get your message across to people with whom you socialize. No one likes to be in the dark as to what you're feeling, so using your face, eyebrows, cheeks and eyes to express with people around you can be a great way of socializing.

Although expressing your interest or disinterest towards something through facial expressions isn't advisable for situations such as a business deal, but more on that later in this chapter.

**Gestures:**

Simple gestures can hold great importance in everyday lyife. Imagine the following scenarios with someone coming to meet the director of a company in their office.

- The guest knocks and enters the room. The director says, "Welcome, please sit."
- The guest knocks and enters the room. The director smiles and says, "Welcome, Mr. Hendrix, please have a seat."
- The guest knocks and enters the room. The director stands up and waits for the guest to proceed, then shakes his hand and says, "Thank you for coming, Mr. Hendrix. I am glad you could make it." He then motions towards the seat and says,

"Please, have a seat. What would you have, coffee, tea or juice?"

In all of these scenarios, the director is essentially doing the same thing; welcoming his guest into his office. If he simply welcomes his guest, as he did in the first case, he probably wouldn't come off as unwelcoming. But if he enacts the last scenario, the guest automatically feels homely and positive at the response that he has received. Chances are that he already likes the director without even starting a conversation.

**Paralinguistics:**

Paralinguistics refer to speech beyond words such as tone, pauses, stresses, pitch and inflexion. Although we would discuss this point in detail in **"Chapter 4: Tonality"**, yet it is of great importance to highlight that it is not just important what you deliver in your speech, but also how you deliver it.

Every sitcom fan in the world must have seen the legendary tv show, F.R.I.E.N.D.S. which is arguably the funniest tv show in history. But if you actually focus on their dialogues, they are pretty much average or better than average, at best! There is nothing special in what they are saying, but actually what makes it funny is how they are saying it.

Speech in general, and humor in specific, centers upon your paralinguistic approach to a dialogue.

**Body posture:**

Your body posture has developed over the span of years. Many of us know that they have to work on it (guilty as charged) but never get around to doing so. But its importance becomes highlighted whenever we meet new people or go for an interview. The way you sit, hold eye contact, stand or walk affects how people perceive your character. For example, puffing up your chest has symbolically been accepted as a symbol of pride while fidgeting with your hands is considered an expression of nervousness.

A study conducted by Columbia and Harvard University suggests that sitting in expansive and powerful poses can increase your appetite for risk to up to 45% as compared to sitting in a constricted pose. This percentage is definitely something to consider while dealing with the people around you.

# 3 major body language groups and their identification

Since people's tone and body language go hand in hand when we try to read them, so I will teach you this art in **"Chapter 4: Tonality."** Over here, I will outline some basic body language groups of people that are quite common everywhere in the world. This will help you classify the people around you systematically into 3 major groups.

You can observe the body language of people around you and try to find what makes them friendly, authoritative, shy or confident. Doing so will teach you tidbits to work on your own character. If someone's body language meets the criterions below, you can get a helpful insight into their mind using the information given.

**A powerful body language:**

People who are mentally strong and wish to assert their power over others tend to sit upright. They walk with purpose even if they aren't going anywhere in particular. When they talk, they like keeping their voice and tone louder or equal to the person that they are sitting with. They often keep their responses short and to the point.

A person who thinks of himself as a powerful character might hold strong eye contact with you if he perceives you to be competition or might not even spare a glance at you if you aren't. Powerful people like having their personal space and often sit afar. Research suggests that such people prefer coffee as their favorite drink.

**A friendly body language:**

A friendly or welcoming body language always includes a smile. This is a point that you should note for your own benefit that a smile goes a long way in establishing any relationship. Nobody wants to be friends with someone who is always gloomy or sad. People like to surround themselves with happy characters and being friendly comes with smiling most of the time while interacting with people.

Friendly people use touch as a way of expression as well. Research suggests that most females use touch as a form of expression for caring, empathy and love.

Friendly people also like to sit close to others and talk in a manner that keeps the discussion alive and fluent. It is a basic character of every friendly person that they are easy to talk to. You might even find them fetching for three different topics in the same sentence because they know how to keep the discourse alive.

**A shy body language:**

Shy people tend to sit in closed postures. They are also very weak in maintaining eye contact and often look at the ground while they talk. Such people twirl with their fingers, fidget and toil around with the crockery while they eat. While sitting on a chair, they often cross their legs under it or clasp their hands in their lap.

Sitting in a hunched manner is also regarded as being outwardly shy. Shy people speak softly and timidly and often keep their replies short which makes it very hard to keep a conversation up with them.

# "What sort of body language should I have?"

This is a very good question, and the answer is: none in particular! You do not always have to be friendly or welcoming. It is not always in your best interest to be expressive in terms of facial expressions because of business reasons.

In tricky scenarios where we don't know which side to take but we have to, it is highly advisable to sit down with both parties alternatively and listen to their side of the story. Understanding both sides completely and realizing the benefits and issues of choosing both options can help you decide on the better option for yourself.

In such a scenario, you should never immediately express like, dislike, love, hatred, suspicion or amazement. Keep your face dead and read what the other person feels like instead. Your best chance at getting a good look into both parties is if none of them know which side you are on and that can only happen if you express nothing while talking to both of them.

Another example of avoiding facial expressions could be during business deals. Expressing immediate liking for an offer will definitely reduce your chance of negotiating a better deal.

We have already decided in **"Chapter 2: Mindset Shift"** that we are everything at the same time. We are fluid and now it is our responsibility to make sure that we comprehend the situation in the best manner and choose what our body language should be for any person.

Body language is not rigid, but can vary for all the different kinds of people that we know. In your business dealings, you would always want to sound and look powerful and authoritative. Remember, that it does not require you to be rude or unwelcoming. As given in the example where a guest comes to meet a company director in his office, the director welcomes him and stands up in respect probably because the guest is a potential client. Now imagine that the person entering his office is his own assistant, would he ever do that?

Understand your relationship with the other person before opting for what sort of body language you should have. Now, coming back to the three examples or groups of body languages that I mentioned above. Chances are that you thought that the powerful body language was something negative and should be despised, but understand that the only reason powerful people opt for it is that it serves them the best.

Similarly, being outwardly shy can help you a lot if you're willing to come off as harmless and want to get some sympathy. I wouldn't advise you to ever be shy, but I just explained a possible positive impact that could come out of it.

Now coming to the friendly body language; that should be the "factory settings" to your body. Learn and master the art of being friendly except when the situation requires you to be otherwise. Do not ever think, "Should I be friendly?" But think, "Are there any reasons not to be?"

If you find no reason at all to be bold with someone, do not ever act that way with them. You want most of the people around you to believe that you are a nice person who is easy to talk to and are welcoming in your approach. That is how you will get to make great friends in your personal life and clients in the business world.

**A few tips to come off as a friendly bloke:**

Here are a few great tips to seem friendly to the people around you. Work on them and learn to include them in your life. This should be your signature character unless explicitly required otherwise.

- Always sit upright.
- Keep a smile most of the time. (Not always, please! That's creepy; just try keeping it to a comfortable level.)
- Incorporate a hand gesture into your speech. Do not play with all the crazy gestures that you can find around the globe. Just motioning with your hand while you talk can be a good way of bringing conviction into your speech.
- Talk like you're sure of what you are saying.
- Nod at regular intervals while you listen to people.
- Listen closely, then if you wish to agree, repeat the same thing that they said in your own words. Remember not to be too people-pleasing. It's okay to disagree with people in a modest way.
- Learn to disagree democratically. A great tip for doing that is by saying: "Yeah, I agree. But…" This way, you don't come off too strong in disagreement and manage to get your point across as well. (More on this in **"Chapter 5: Conversations."**)
- Never fidget with your hands and fingers. If you ever catch yourself doing that, stop right there and then.

These are a few basic tips that will help you not only look friendly but also confident, and confidence is key, my friend! Never be unsure of yourself and what you are saying. Yes, you might be wrong about something and talking with conviction as well. But that's way better than being right but not confident enough to express your viewpoint.

So, reread these tips again and write down those traits or tips in your secret notebook that you believe lack in your character. Over the course of the coming days, keep it in your mind to work on these tips while talking to the people already in your life. Remember that we will work on making new friends in **"Chapter 6: Social Momentum and Calibration."** Right now, practice this on your existing friends and family. This will help you when you actually go out to socialize with new people.

Once you get the hang of a point, tick it off the list. Having such a list is beneficial as you are mentally working towards the completion of a written task which has many times greater efficacy than a casual reminder that you might have placed in your head.

# Chapter 4

# Tonality

Humans are considered to be the pioneers of Earth; the smartest species that has evolved its method of living from the dark ages up till today when everything is a mere click away. It has been a huge development for our race, and the cornerstone of this development is nothing but the human ability to speak.

What sets humans apart and above from all other species is the ability to speak languages and convey their feelings, thoughts and emotions effectively. None of our development would have been possible without the ability of speech. It is not our brains that led to this upbringing of such a diversified and beautiful society, but our ability to convey what these brains hold.

But even when everyone knows how to speak, some orators have the ability to convey far more strongly than others. Their voice has an effect that very few have; something that makes the listeners yearn for more. Their voice has this irresistible feeling to it that whatever is conveyed through it, people want to listen more and believe whatever it conveys.

If you look at some of the best orators in recent history; Martin Luther King, Mohandas Gandhi, John F. Kennedy, Nelson Mandela, Barack Obama, all these people had or have the ability to use their voice in the best manner possible. They not only said the most meaningful words, but also knew how to and when to convey them.

Your tone and way of speaking goes a long way into how people comprehend your speech. Even if you have the best words to say and the greatest insight into the topic that you're speaking about, if you do not know or learn the art of using your voice in the correct way, then your arguments, points and speech would be useless.

**Owning your voice as an instrument:**

Music is nothing but positive sound. People prefer to hear music that relaxes them. They want to hear more of it because they get used to that feeling that music gives them; of a transient state of calm and poise.

Imagine if you could train your own voice to have that effect on people. As I said, music is nothing but positive sound, so if you can train your own voice, you could be music to someone's ears.

Own this instrument that you call your voice box and learn to play it in the most effective way possible. If we consider your voice box to be a guitar, then you have probably just been strumming random strings up till now. But with the tips and techniques that I'll be teaching you in this chapter, you'll learn all the notes and keys and get a hang of the complete instrument if you keep up and incorporate the tips into your own life. Although you can find professional voice coaches that can teach you some great techniques to control your voice one on one, but I will try to cover maximum aspects in this chapter that I can without physically being with you.

Remember to practice these with the existing people in your life before trying them out for making new friends. As I mentioned in the previous chapter as well, that part would come later once we get the hang of our body language, tonality and speech.

# "Does it really matter how I sound as long as I'm saying the truth?"

That's a really important question and something that blinds most of us for a good part of our lives until something clicks to us in a random situation and we realize how wrong we were. Research suggests that words only account for 7% of how we interpret people! Actually, the bulk of our interpretations of people are from body language which rounds to a 55% and tone which represents 30%.

So, your body language and tone definitely are extremely important for conversations and socialization. Another reality that we seem to ignore is that everyone always thinks that they are right!

You need to get used to this reality if you wish to lead a realistic life. There is probably no real truth to anything. There is only conjecture and point of views. The truth for me could be far different from the truth that you believe in just because we have lived two separate lives, seen different things, experienced different emotions, met different people and had different experiences. Because of this, we have accumulated different beliefs over our lifetimes.

Remember in **"Chapter 2: Mindset Shift"** when I asked you to leave all your limiting beliefs behind? I mentioned over there that having limiting beliefs limits your reality. That reality is your truth! If you create a belief about anything, your reality remains confined within that belief. No matter what happens in life, you will always perceive everything within the boundaries of things that you believe in.

Now coming back to truths and point of views. Imagine that there are two friends: Greg and Alan. Greg goes to the moon while Alan stays behind on the Earth. Upon reaching the moon, Greg sees the

Earth above himself while he stood on the surface of the moon. When he comes back and explains it to Alan who was on planet Earth all the time, he makes fun of Greg's theory because he has seen the moon higher up in the sky all his life.

Greg swears that he saw the Earth higher than the moon when he landed there and explains how he had to lift his head up to see it, but only receives sarcasm in return. Who do you think is right out of the two?

None of them and both of them! Their only difference is that of point of view. When you're standing on the moon and under its gravitational field, you'll see the Earth above it. But if you're standing on the Earth and are within its gravitational field, you'll see the moon above it. Both of them are true but wrong at the same time due to their difference in reference; the truth for Greg is the exact opposite to the truth for Alan!

The point that I'm trying to make over here is that in such a situation where there is probably no truth, your chances of making people agree to your reference and point of view is amplified if you learn the art of tonality. No matter how right you are, your opposers will always believe that you are wrong.

This nullifies the aspect that you have to say the truth and the right thing and that it should be enough to make people hear your speech. People do not care about the truth or the right or best thing to say. When their ears lay upon a particular voice which soothes them, they continue hearing it! That's how it goes. It is up to you to make your voice attractive enough for them to want to hear you in the first place. Words, arguments, truth; all of it comes after.

# Controlling your own tonality

Controlling your tonality is the best and most effective way of attracting people to your voice. As I have mentioned above, what you say is important too, but people will only hear it if you say it in a way that they appreciate. That is the only reason that I have put the chapter on conversations after this chapter on tonality.

Your voice box is actually a set of tools that you can hone and sharpen into something great. Each tool brings more and more effectiveness into your speech. Take some time to understand each of them and the plethora of opportunities and benefits that they bring to you and try to incorporate them into your daily lives. It will take some practicing, and as I have mentioned above, you can find a professional voice coach to help you learn the art of tonality. But if you focus hard enough, then this chapter along with some Youtube videos should be enough to at least put you on the right track to conquering your own voice.

**"So, what are my voice tools?"**

As hinted above, you have a complete plethora of tools that you can use to make your voice more attractive and soothing. Here is a list of those tools that all of us possess.

1. **Voice location:**

If you place your hand on your chest, you can actually locate your voice. Although it is a tricky task to explain this to you through the mere use of words, but I'll try my best. Everybody has a location in their body from where their voice originates. Some people tend to speak high up in their nose. This voice is usually attributed to nerds and films have helped telecast this particular voice location in that manner for years now.

Other people tend to speak from the center of their throats. This is much like the factory setting for human beings and is a pretty good option to start with. Speaking from your throat gives you a wide range of pitches and allows some easy access to change-ups in voice location. Even within your throat, you can find different locations for your voice like speaking right up in a shrill voice or going right down into the junction between your throat and diaphragm.

Voice location also affects our voice projection and pitch to a great extent, which may again affect how people view us in the world. Having a really shrill voice can make you sound unauthoritative and weak. But having a deep voice can help you sound authoritative and powerful. Research suggests that we vote for candidates that have a deep voice because we associate depth with power and authority.

The third, and if I may, hardest voice location is the diaphragm. Here, we are talking about some professional stuff. Theatre actors and singers undergo years of training to perfect their stage and singing voices so that they can truly unlock the complete potential in this matter. Undergoing regular voice exercises allows them to have great voice quality and control. Have you ever wondered how theatre actors are able to make their voice reach 1000 people at the same time without having a mic? Well, now you know.

You can watch a few helpful Youtube videos on how to locate your voice in your diaphragm, but I'll help you out with a simple exercise that has been taught to me by different theatre directors that I've had the opportunity to work with. Place your hand on your chest and try taking your voice as deep as you can into your diaphragm; we're talking scary deep over here! You don't have to say anything, a simple "Aaaaaaaa" will suffice. Opening your mouth wide can help you eliminate that urge to speak from your throat.

If you feel some strong vibration from your chest, that means that your voice is originating from your diaphragm. If bulk of the vibrations can be felt from your throat, then you need to keep working on bringing it lower into your diaphragm. This can be a little hard to achieve in the first attempt without anyone there to guide you, but if you keep working on it and watch some pros, you're bound to succeed at this.

Once you're able to succeed in locating your voice in your diaphragm, then slowly increase your volume till the maximum extent without pushing it back to your throat. The louder you can get without hitting your voice into your throat, the broader your spectrum of voice and pitch is. Regular voice exercise can help you master your own voice and give you the ability to play with different sounds and volumes.

## 2. Timbre:

Timbre refers to your voice quality. In easy and non-technical terms, it refers to how your voice feels. Some people's voice just seems to cut through ear drums. It makes you want to kill them, doesn't it? It's like you see these people and you wish you could hang yourself from a ceiling fan.

While on the other hand, there are people that just have this soft, smooth and rich voice that's so luscious that everything they say feels like chocolate. Your goal is to learn how to speak like those people. You want your words to soothe others. Learn to be soft in the way you speak. Subtle, but smart and firm. Being soft does not mean that you're unsure of what to say. It just means that you're not coming off too strong in stating your opinion.

If you naturally do not have a really soft and smooth voice, then it isn't something to fret over. This is where acceptance comes in. Learn to differentiate between having a problem and not having an advantage. Having a soft voice is an advantage, but not having one is not a problem.

Take ownership of your voice and do what you can to benefit from it. Slow down and enunciate each word completely and you'll enhance the rich factor of your voice to a good extent.

3. **Prosody:**

Prosody can be defined as your ability to stress and pause, creating your own rhythmicity to your voice. Everybody has their own rhythm of speaking and that's fine until you start throwing each sentence into the same template of rhythm that you're accustomed to.

Many people have a problem of speaking each statement as if it's a question and frankly, it gets irritating. The last word of each of their statements ends up with a virtual question mark that leaves the listener baffled of what to expect. It not only bamboozles your listener, but also shows your uncertainty about yourself and your statements.

Another problem that I see with so many people around me is that they do not vary their tone at all. They say everything in such an expressionless manner that it is hard to distinguish their statements from questions and requests from sarcasm. Talking to such a person can be a nightmare so avoid doing that at all costs.

Your tone also speaks volumes about your character. Happy people have chirpy and jolly tones while sad people have grim tones. Manliness is associated with deep tones while femininity is associated with shrill tones. This is how people can judge you through the manner in which you speak.

Humor is also highly related to prosody. At this moment, I'd like to refer one of the most iconic characters in tv history: Chandler Bing! We all love him; the extremely funny yet unusually awkward guy that says the most random dialogues in the most hilarious way. In comedy, it's not so much about what you're saying, but how you're saying it.

There are some people who just make everybody laugh at each thing that they say. Even before they've uttered a word, people get ready to be amused. You could just see their face and start laughing because you associate them to laughter. These people are often saying average daily lines in manners that most others can't emulate or copy. These are pauses, stresses and intonations.

For anyone who knows Chandler Bing, you can for sure imagine him saying: "Could I *be* any funnier?" Notice the stress on the word "be". That simple stress makes it so much more powerful and iconic. You could say it that way in front of 10 people and at least 3 will register the character that you're trying to copy. That is the power of using prosody to create for yourself an icon that people recognize you by.

### 4. Pace:

Pace is very important to maintain the digestibility of your speech. Everyone takes different amounts of time to process what you're saying in their head and truly understand it. Do not waste all your time and energy by telling people stuff that their mind probably isn't registering in the first place, or even if it is, you're not giving them ample time to process it long enough, so they can remember it later.

Some people are naturally fast-talkers while others hurry on to their words when they are excited. It is a natural thing to do, but honestly, you're better off without it. Your goal should be to make your words understandable and digestible to anyone that you talk to. If you're an English-speaking person, you'll come across loads of foreigners that speak your language, but take some extra time into processing what you say and then answering it.

One tip that you could use to train your voice for a better pace would be to imagine that you're talking to a foreigner. Speak at a pace that even they would be able to cooperate with. Don't get too slow that it becomes irritating for the listeners, but just enough that they don't have to wonder what you're saying.

Another good tip is to vary your pace while you speak. Slowing down at a particular point can have a really dramatic effect on your speech and makes it attractive for the listeners. Adding pauses can further arouse suspense in your listeners and can help you gain some valuable attention.

### 5. Silence:

Silence is another tool that many people tend to forget. No, I'm not advising you to say nothing, but I'm talking about the moments of nothingness in your speech. People love contrast. Adding a pause between your speech and just remaining silent during it can have such a lovely effect on your listeners.

Especially when telling a story, if you're stopping for a couple of seconds just to arouse the suspense in your listeners, they'll be dying to know what happens next. There is nothing wrong with having a few moments of silence. Do not fill them with "um" and "ah." These fillers make it clear to your listeners that you've either forgotten what you wanted to say or aren't sure how to put it. You would always want to look like you're in control and know what you're talking about. So, cut these fillers and add in some useful silence to your speech.

### 6. Pitch:

Many people don't realize how effective changing your pitch can be while you communicate with people. So much, that if you change your pitch, you might even change the meaning of what you say. Take, for instance, the following sentence:
"Where did you put my keys?"

Say it in a deep and authoritative tone first and you'll comprehend it in a manner of question. You might imagine a working husband asking this from his stay-at-home wife minutes before leaving for work.
Now say the same sentence in a higher pitch, taking your voice up to the edge of your throat. You might imagine it to be said now in accusative tone. You could imagine it to be said by one sibling to the other moments before a dreadful fight or argument.

Variation in pitch is again a key instrument in making your voice attractive. It is another art altogether to understand which pitch to use for which scenario. Business talks require deep notes and pitches while arguments often end up in high ones. Observe the people around you and how they react and process to different pitches and you might notice a pattern that would help you.

### 7. Volume:

Lastly, comes volume. This tool is effective through its variation as well. At all times, you would wish to be audible to all the people that you're talking to. Some people say that they are naturally shy or low-talkers, but in fact, that is just due to our years of conditioning ourselves to believe that we are a limited reality. I keep going back to the points raised in **"Chapter 2: Mindset Shift"** because it is just so important for you to learn social intelligence, but I'd like to quote it again at this moment.

When you left your limiting beliefs behind, you also eradicated beliefs such as: "I am naturally too shy to talk loudly." You are not too anything to be too anything! The easiest thing to change in life is yourself, believe me. Because in this process, you only need to convince one soul and that is yourself. If you are truly able to convince yourself to bring a change in life, then that change will come no matter how much people or the environment wishes to stop it.

So, start speaking confidently and loud enough for people to hear. But on the other end of the spectrum, a very common issue with people is that they speak a little too loudly. The aim isn't to make people's ear drums bleed. Try being audible to the person that is farthest from you without making the person that's the closest feel uncomfortable. A good technique to learn is sound direction. While speaking to a large group, keep your face directed at them.

This would help your sound waves reach them better without colliding off the walls of the room and reducing sound quality. Also, if you are talking to two people simultaneously with one of them sitting beside you and the other in front of you, then try keeping your face towards the one sitting in front as he is farther away from you as compared to the one who is sitting right beside you. This way, your voice throw will effectively reach both people at the same time. If you keep your face towards the person sitting beside you, not only will your voice be unable to reach the guy in front, but you might make the guy sitting beside you uncomfortable with your noise.

While speaking loudly, you can change up your volume and make people really focus on what you have to say. This effect can be really hot in case of some romantic speech too, but only if it's done the right way. If you think you're sounding creepy when you do that, then it's better to practice it beforehand until the next time you pull that out on a date. More on dating in **"Chapter 8: Dating Perfection."**

Do not be predictable in your speech but learn how to be unexpected in how you deliver your speech. Volume can help you do that.

## "How can I read the tonality and body language of others?"

Let's just agree to this: we are all surrounded by "snakes"! Although this term is the new thing for teenagers, but if you are still unaware of it, I'll explain it to you. A snake is a person that is dishonest, fake, two-faced and not a true friend at all. These people will show you that they honestly care about you and your well-being, but they couldn't actually care less for you!

All they want is to just be able to spend some time with you, get the hottest gossip from your side, and then spill it over to other people that they talk to. A very interesting insight was given to me by a female friend regarding judging the tone of other women. She said, "Higher the pitch, the more she's been a bitch!"

Now, I would like to remind you that this is a personal opinion of an individual and certainly not a theory or research, but it's a thought worth processing, nonetheless. The point here, is that it's so vital for us to read and understand people beyond their words.

A research from the "Journal of Nonverbal Behavior" suggests mid-adolescent people find it the hardest to judge people according to their tone. But this tool is not just important for teenagers, but also for adults of all ages.

Sometimes we are sitting in a meeting and we're out there floating an idea that people are initially hesitant to comment on. We might be debating if we should pursue it further and explain its benefits to all that are present, but is it worth a shot?

You might have gone up to this girl and flirted with her. Now, you're weighing in your next move and the only way that you can do that is if you are effectively able to decipher her body language. This part of the chapter focuses on all these aspects that you have to take into account while reading people. If you follow each of these, I'm sure you'll be able to read people in the most effective manner.

One thing that I would request you, is to not be too analytical and leave prerequisites and past beliefs about people behind yourself. We have spent a lot of time on beliefs but I will keep reminding you that when you started your journey with me, you promised to leave all your limiting beliefs behind and this is one of them. Look at everyone in a new and neutral way and all these techniques will work the best for you.

   1. **The face:**

People's face says a lot about them. You can get a good idea about their character if you focus long enough on how they look. Frown lines on their foreheads can speak volumes about them. Such people are often spending loads of time thinking and worrying about stuff.

This might even be a cue of their aging or premature aging due to tension. Crow's feet are wrinkles on the edge of people's eyes. They are usually attributed to people who smile and laugh a lot, leaving permanent lines etched on their face.

Other than these two main-stream and permanent features, there are other things that you can be cautious about. A clenched jaw usually depicts tension while pursed lips show anger or bitterness on their behalf. If you focus well enough, you'll find many little tidbits which would provide you insight into people's mindset.

2. **Clothing:**

Clothing is also a very important aspect of people's character. Again, do not be too analytical on this aspect. This is more a choice than a mentality statement. But on a broad spectrum, this can give you a very good idea about what others perceive the meeting to be.

If they choose to wear formal clothes with well-polished shoes, that means they perceive this meeting to be business-level. Their choice of wearing or not wearing a tie and a blazer can also explain to you the extent of how formal they believe it to be. On the other hand, if they choose to wear a t-shirt and jeans with sneakers, this shows their casual approach towards you.

Again, for people with a deep style-sense, wearing a cotton-jeans with a tucked-in formal shirt and dress shoes is far from wearing the same outfit with casual loafers or sneakers. Now, judging people's intentions for your meeting based on such minute details might not be a very good idea while meeting such characters that personally don't care that much about their clothing, or do not have a strong sense of style, or an extensive wardrobe. But for someone who knows the dressing-game well enough, this might hint you as to what this meeting means to them.

For women, this can be a lot easier since casual and formal clothing are quite obvious in their regard. Risky outfits can also give you an idea about what they're expecting out of the day or meeting.

### 3. Posture:

The posture that people adopt while socializing with you is a very important thing to consider. Are they sitting openly or in a closed manner? As mentioned above, the former shows confidence and power while the latter depicts frailty.

Another important aspect is where do these people lean to while talking to you. Research suggests that we lean towards people that we are attracted to and away from people that we despise. It is a very natural reaction and an authentic method of accessing the mental state of people. The distance that they keep with you is also a matter of interest while considering body language. Lesser the distance, more the attraction and greater the distance, lesser the attraction.

I'll mention a few other tidbits for your convenience. Having crossed arms and legs can be a sign of defensiveness or something that people wish to hide. Other habits like lip-biting and foot-tapping during conversation can show how nervous the other person is.

### 4. The tone:

A study was published by Michael Kraus from Yale University, with the title, "Voice-Only Communication Enhances Empathetic Accuracy." In this study, Kraus found that listening to someone's voice alone is a far better method of judging how they feel as compared to their facial expressions. This means that you can get a better idea of how someone feels on voice call rather than watching their video. (Facetime will tell you otherwise.)

The next time you talk to someone, notice how their voice feels. Is it soothing and soft? Does that make you wish to hear them more? Or is it just harsh and abrasive? Some people are so whiny that this character etches on to their tone of voice and you can actually guess that they must be really whiny in real life.

Another study conducted by Nielson Norman Group shows that while purposefully using two different tones of voice on their website, "the casual, conversational and enthusiastic tones performed the best." This gives us an insight that people like this tone and you should strive for adopting it as well.

5. **Gut feeling:**

Your gut feeling can tell you a lot about a person. It often happens that our mind picks up on a nuance that went by too fast for us to capture properly. But it is due to this that we get a bad gut feeling about some people. It is noteworthy that this might not act as a great criterion for those who always suffer from having a bad gut feeling about everything.

6. **The vibe:**

The vibe that people give off is simply their emotional energy. How do they make you feel when you're around? Are they easy to be with or do they make you emotionally uncomfortable? The feeling of their handshake or touch can also make your mind register certain details about their character. A firm handshake is often regarded as a positive in someone's character but a loose handshake without making eye-contact can depict shyness on their behalf.

7. **Decipher the smile:**

Although each smile is perceived to be positive, yet this is a common misconception among people. We have made smiling too much of a cliché that people are just doing that for no reason at all. See if people's smile goes with their eyes as well. Often, you will decipher fake smiles if their eye-lids don't lower at all during the process. I personally do not think it's possible not to have your eyes become smaller when you are genuinely smiling.

Also, a short-lived smile with pursed lips can show a form of acknowledgment and not of a happy and positive character. That's something that we naturally do when we see people walk past and we wish to register their presence. Another type of unorthodox smile is when people are smiling without a proper cause while their eyes scan the complete room nervously; this shows uneasiness on people's behalf. If you wish to make such people feel comfortable, you can try talking to them and including them in group conversations. As soon as they start feeling included, this sensation would slowly alleviate.

8. **Read the eyes:**

Eyes speak volumes about how people feel. It is a common saying that, "Eyes are windows to the soul." And that is quite true in application. Our eyes are probably the one thing that we can't control consciously if we wish to hide our emotions. The reason is that our pupils biologically grow and shrink in response to things that we like or dislike.

Here's what Donna Van Netten, the Body Language Dr. says in her interview with Marcel Schwantes about the expression of feelings with eyes:

"Pupils (of the eye) change under certain conditions--especially when they are triggered by our emotions. When we're attracted to or like something, they grow; when we don't, they shrink."

If you focus hard enough on the eyes of people and are able to decipher them, this one tip is something that can not lie. You will most definitely be able to see the pupils of people dilate and constrict while you speak, but it will take you some practice. Doing so with people who have bigger eyes gives you a better chance as compared to trying it with the Chinese. But I'm sure you can give it a go!

**Task for the secret notebook:**

I will be coming back to your secret notebook again and again to remind you to write down your mental tasks. This was a very informative chapter, and to be honest, it's not easy to process all of this at once. Chances are that you'll forget what I taught you in this chapter after you wake up tomorrow morning.

So, use this chance to write down what you think you should work on in terms of your tone, body language and posture. Was there something that clicked in your mind while reading this? Writing it down means mentally registering that you will take out the time or mental energy to work on this.

# Chapter 5

# Conversations

Now that you have learned how to mediate your body language and posture along with all the tools that you could use to project your voice in the most effective manner, I believe that it is time that we move on to the most dreaded factor in Social Intelligence: speech!

Let's just agree to it: we all have been scared before talking to certain people or about certain subjects. It's normal to feel timid or not up to the task while conversing with people. My late debating coach used to say:

"Man, even today I'm so scared of speaking on stage that I hold a blank page in my hand just for moral support. If it wasn't for this page, I'd be shitting my pants!"

That's when I realized, even the greatest orators are scared of orating. It's such an arduous task that it even overwhelms the experts in the field.

But that's only because speech is such a powerful tool. There is nothing that can be simultaneously both so dangerous and beautiful than the words that leave your mouth. Try as you may, but you can never name another tool that has been the cause of wars, peace, love, hatred, defeats, victories, happiness, sorrow- and every damn thing in between!

We all can see how effective this weapon is, but still we're scared of using it. Why? Because we consider ourselves monkeys holding a machinegun; we know that we hold something really powerful, but we don't trust ourselves not to shoot our own brains out with the weapon.

Understand that this is your weapon to conquer the world. The greatest men in history, all of them knew how to use their tongue, and that's why they rose to such heights. Accept this weapon and I will teach you how to use it. Once you get the feeling of ownership to this weapon, no matter where you go and how unhospitable the people around you are, you'll still feel safe and in control because you'd trust your tongue to always come up with something witty, meaningful and acceptable.

Unfortunately, the control to this weapon is something that is even ignored in our education systems. We are always willing to make students cram information, but how to present it is considered something that they are supposed to figure out on their own. There was a great piece published in The Atlantic by a high school teacher, Paul Barnwill. He wrote: "I came to realize that conversational competence might be the single most over-looked skill we fail to teach (to students.)"

In this chapter, I'll cover all the basics of how to make conversations with people including initiation and continuation. We will try to understand why arguments occur and how to avoid them along with secrets to becoming a part of larger group conversations.

**Conversations are the basis of every relationship:**

Understanding this statement will help you accept the ground realities in life far better than you might be right now. No matter how funny, loving and interesting you might think you are, unless you can show that to people, it's of no use. All of these traits are like a treasure that this badass pirate stashed under the Earth but no one could ever find it.

You need to show that treasure to everyone. You need to believe that the world is waiting on your individual gift to appear in front of everyone. We all are experts at something, now it is our responsibility to show that to the world.

Whenever we talk to people, it's like we're establishing a metal link with them. Understand that we're growing a chain of relationships in life. When we meet more people through that first person, we add more metal links to the one that has already been established previously.

Talking to the same person repeatedly and doing it right strengthens the metal link that we have with them. But if we're not adept at the art of speech, it is only a matter of time before we say something that compromises the strength of our metal link with that person, causing it to break. This has the potential of us losing all the other links that we had established on the basis of the first one.

It is due to this reason that each relationship is important in life. You do not want to be that person that's known to be choosy in people that they interact with. Whether you like or dislike a person, do not break your link with them. You can maintain a weak link; meaning that whenever you see them, you just say hi!

But you never know just how important a link could prove to be in the future, so breaking it is not a good option. Every person in the world can be of use to you at a particular situation in life. Remember that you do not always need good people on your side; some situations require you to have a bad guy in your corner too.

So, be that person that no one shits about behind their backs; that people either like or have neutral feelings about. Your goal in life should be to always increase the length of your chain.

It is important to understand that there isn't a single person in the entire universe that isn't despised by anyone. Despite that, many people look as if the whole world appreciates who they are. These people are actually the ones who are wary of the secret of never letting their chain of socialization break from any point.

# Sins of speaking

Before we move on to what and how you should speak, it is important to rule out what you should never! For this purpose, I will be enlisting some sins of speech; the acts that should never be incurred while you speak to anyone about anything.

- **Gossiping:**

So, I was talking to this female friend of mine about how women gossip so much that if you told them a story about a kid falling from their bicycle, then they would tell the same story to other women like: David Beckham ran over a kid on his monster truck that did a 360 cartwheel after the collision and landed on its roof.

After my friend took much offense from this exaggerated comment (yeah, seriously, how am I even teaching you how to speak?), she told me that men, like myself, are equally prone to gossiping. She was of the view that although men and women have different topics of gossip, yet men are not far behind from women in terms of this act.

When I started observing the people around me, I found her point to be quite valid. Yes, telling your sick stories about the women that you've been with does, in fact, come under the gossiping banner, guys.

Rid yourself of this horrendous act. Gossip is nothing but a waste of time and a form of entertainment. If you gossip too much, the weight that your words hold is lessened to a great extent as people find it hard to trust you with their privacy and details. This will make them reluctant to talk and express with you.

- **Judging:**

Oh, boy! How many times have we judged people for doing the same things that we do in every day life. "Look at that guy; staying at home while his wife goes to work. Such a loser." But if we face unemployment at any time and have to stay behind, we can find millions of very venerable reasons to be in the comfortable confines of our homes, drink some coffee and watch the NBA.

Something that makes people highly uncomfortable is the feeling of being judged by others. If you're famous for doing that, they won't take you into confidence for telling you about their life.

- **Negativity:**

Some people are so negative that they make you want to hit your own head in a wall. You could be talking about the most randomly beautiful thing in the world, and they'll find a way to look at it negatively. You could be saying something like: "HEY, YOU WON THE LOTTERY!" and they'd probably reply with, "Meh, it's all a scam anyways."

Learn to find the positive in everything. Be glad for being alive and with the people that surround you. No one wants to talk to people that look at everything in a gloomy manner.

- **Complaining:**

It's as simple as that: stop whining! I understand that your life might really suck, but people can only have so much of an adult crying and whining about their life all day long. People wish to surround themselves with happiness, not sorrow.

Even if you really trust someone close to you to always listen and understand your problems, deep down inside, they are probably sick of hearing all of that if you won't shut up about it. It is okay to talk about your problems, but not always! Don't spread your sorrow into everyone else.

- **Excuses:**

We are never wrong, are we? I mean, have you ever heard a single person in your entire life who agrees that a traffic accident that they were a part of was their own fault. Because if you have, I'd like to meet and congratulate them on being the only person that I know who's achieved this feat.

Do not put your shortcomings on everything and everyone else. If you couldn't do something or achieve a goal or aim, it's fine to agree that it's your own fault. Stop making pointless excuses about your conditions. There have always been people who have done things that you were trying to do in far more arduous conditions than yours.

Learn to accept that because people hate someone who doesn't own their shortcomings.

- **Exaggeration:**

Nothing wrong with a little exaggeration, right? I mean if your pressure cooker exploded, it's equivalent to saying that you burnt your whole kitchen up.

Wrong! Tell stories the way that they happened and not the way that would make them sound crazier. Yes, that might get you some useful attention, but it all goes downhill once people find out that it's your habit to do so. After that, whenever they talk to you, they'll probably be thinking that every story that you tell them is more a lie than the truth.

- **Dogmatism:**

For those of you who do not know what this word means, it's a term used for people that are too assertive in the opinions that they have. Please, do not hold opinions as if they are facts, no matter how strongly you believe in them.

Ever wonder why many people hate majority of the feminists? It's because many feminists seem to come off as too strong and assertive in what they believe in. That makes other feminists' case weak as well as people tend to generalize them as an assertive group. Despite your saying some meaningful stuff, if you're saying it as if it's a holy scripture and not having the patience to let others disagree with it, then people are most likely going to avoid speaking to you no matter how much sense you make while you do so.

- **Giving opinions when people haven't asked for them:**

I can not stress just how much people hate this act. If they haven't asked your opinion about something, please do not give it to them. This makes them feel like they are being judged which makes them uncomfortable.

Let's say someone's telling you about their new job offer and the pay, if they aren't asking you to give your opinion about it, please do not tell them how you think the pay is too less or the work sucks! Your opinion does not matter over here. It isn't about you and you shouldn't make it so.

# Cornerstones of effective speech

Now that we have gone through all the sins of speaking, I would like to proceed to the cornerstones of powerful and effective speech. If you're able to master these traits, people are going to like what you say no matter how much they disagree with you on an individual level. These points are something to always remember while you're speaking with anyone from any background.

- **Honesty:**

I have already mentioned the term "snakes" in this book, so I need not elaborate further as to why you shouldn't be one of them. Always be honest in what you say. If you don't mean something, then don't say it. Your fake persona can only last for so long and before you know it, people will read you for being the person that you are.

Understand that being honest doesn't mean saying mean things to people's face. That is still, and always will be, referred to as being plain rude. Honesty means to always be ready to give your honest yet softly-worded opinions only when asked for on a subject. It also means that you're not backbiting on people. As I mentioned in the part of "Conversations are the basis of relationships", if you do not like a person, just say hi to them, ask them about their day and move on. After they're gone, you do not need to be discussing how much you hate them with other people.

As I said, gossip is everywhere and when that person realizes how dishonest you are, he'll start hating you, breaking your metal link with him in the process.

- **Authenticity:**

Always be authentic in the information that you're giving to people. Do not just float everything that you heard to people that you know. Before giving people some sort of information, make sure that you're getting it from the correct and closest source.

If you just happened to get wind of something, then it's better to give other people a disclaimer that you're not sure if this piece of information is correct. It does not make you an invalid person if you tell people that you're not sure about something. But telling them that you are and then ending up being wrong about the subject is not only going to make people dislike you, but will also embarrass you along the way.

- **Integrity:**

Treat people with respect so they can treat you the same way. It is up to us to define the limitations of every relationship. Just leaving the limits up to fate can get you into a lot of trouble.

Never compromise on your own social integrity. This means that you shouldn't express your vulnerability in front of people that you do not trust. This has become a new trend among men and women to express how vulnerable and weak they are in order to gain attention, but you ought to stay away from that. Always maintain your integrity as an individual at all times.

- **Love:**

I don't mean romantic love **(more on that in Chapter 8: Dating Perfection)**, but your overall persona of being positive, happy, soft and loving. The choice and your selection of words can have a great impact on the people around you. Treat people regardless of their age as equals and see how that positively impacts your life.

Being loving in this manner will allow you to be very easy to talk to for everyone and will help you create magical conversations.

# Initiating conversations

I know, these are dreadful! The ability to confidently initiate conversations with anyone is highly restricted to a select few. But let me assure you that if you implement the tips and mindset that I'll try inculcating in this chapter, you'll find this task to be far easier than you expect. Try practicing these on the people already present in your life before you go trying them out on strangers. As I mentioned before as well, we will come to that part in **"Chapter 6: Social Momentum and Calibration."**

Here are a few tips for initiating a conversation with just about anyone.

- **Self-confidence:**

The first and foremost point to consider for any conversation is self-confidence. The only reason that one feels nervous while going up to someone and talking to them is if they are scared of what perception the other person might take of them. Be confident in your own skin; only then can you be outwardly confident enough to talk to people.

Let me ask you this question: do you like yourself as a person? Remember when I asked you in **"Chapter 2: Mindset Shift"** to write down the answer to whether you would want to be friends with your own self?

If you answered that you like yourself truly and would want to be friends, then feel confident that others would want the same. If you wrote that you dislike yourself or that you wouldn't want to be friends with yourself, that's fine. You actually just made things a lot easier for yourself because you outlined the problems that you probably were facing while socializing.

If you wrote that you wouldn't want to be friends with your own self because you are too shy, or speak too less, or are too boring, you just outlined the broad reasons why you're facing a problem socializing with other people. Because chances are, that these are the exact issues that hinder you while interacting with others. Now, it is your responsibility to work on this factor because it is absolutely integral for you and your Social Intelligence.

Work on accepting your own self and become a person that you would enjoy being with. Would you want to hang out with someone who likes to stay alone at home and watch tv all day or someone who's up for going to that bowling alley despite not knowing how to throw a damn bowling ball? Learn to teach yourself to be fun and that's how you will grow in self-confidence in your social sphere.

Once that is done, you'll feel confident that you are a fun person and chances are that whoever you're about to talk to, will like you and enjoy your company.

- **Be the first one out of the gate**

I once saw this meme on Facebook about how my way of flirting is to look at women really long and hard and hope that they are confident enough to come up and talk to me. Well, that's most of us. Being the first one out of the gate is something that we rarely ever do.

If you're not willing to try this out, you're reducing your chances at socialization by manifold because you're entrusting luck to help you socialize. You're waiting for a scenario where you wouldn't have to go through that single awkward minute of beginning a conversation with someone randomly, and chances are that the people around you would feel the same.

A great way to battle this issue is to think, "What's the worst that could happen to me right now?" Worst case scenario: this person that you're trying to talk to would not want to talk to you back. Well, news flash: they aren't doing so right now as well!

So, stop overthinking about all of this. This is one of those moments where I want you to just leave your mind out of it and just go and say "hi" or "hello." You'll have these awkward ten seconds where your body feels that something unusual is happening because you've been living the life of a cooped-up cat that likes to sit on the sofa and watch tv series that they don't really understand, but you'll get over the feeling. It fades away as fast as it comes.

These first words are the floodgate, if you open it, everything else just flows after that.

- **Skip the small talk:**

This small talk is the basis of awkward conversations. Because in your mind, you're always fretting over whether you should say, "Hi!", "Hey", or "Hello" and "What's up?" or "What'cha doin'?", and "How are you?" or "How do you feel?" Before you realize it, your mind's creating new words and expressions that you've never even heard before and the conversation has turned into something quite awkward and dreadful!

By the time you're done with this small talk and need to talk about something meaningful now, you have no idea how that happens. And then comes the dreaded awkward pause. Instead, you should greet people and even ask them how they are, but then move on to something meaningful and compact. You might even ask them a personal question. I know that sounds weird, but you'll be amazed at how people respond so openly to others that are confident enough to just ask.

Another way might be to ask their opinion about anything. You could tell them how you've been reading about this topic and the author feels this way but you disagree. Now ask them what their opinion is on the matter.

Now, don't go asking them about stuff like aliens or time travel. You're just making them anxious by bringing up something so technical. Instead, talk about basic stuff like "Where are you from?" or "Do you like the summers?" or "When was the last time you went for vacations and where?"

The beauty of this technique is that the answers to these questions will always be something unique and personal; stuff that you have never heard before because it's different for everyone. That's why you should ask something meaningful and compact instead of the pointless small talk. Nobody can like you or enjoy your company simply because you're good at saying hi.

I have mentioned a few ice breaking questions for skipping small talk in **"Chapter 8: Dating Perfection."**

- **Find the "ME TOOs"**

You've probably heard this before and that is because this is one of the cornerstones of effective and prolonged conversations. While talking to people for the first time, explore different topics and see what makes them click. Which topic makes their eyes light up with enthusiasm and recognition? When you see them getting excited about a topic, that's something that you should discuss more because it is evident that they enjoy speaking about it.

Finding mutual similarities with people is really important. It might even be something as simple as you both liking the summers. This is basic, but opens a whole world of possible subtopics to discuss, like going to the beach, wearing comfortable clothes or reasons why you hate the winters.

We often say that we somehow "click" with a person. This click happens because we find something common with them which makes us feel comfortable and homely. Although having differences and matters of contrast isn't a bad thing either; it is often said that two absolutely similar people could never be in a long-lasting relationship. This is because when two people have contrasting elements to their characters, then one person not being able to do something is compensated by the other person doing it. If two stubborn people are in a relationship, they would probably part ways very soon because no one would be willing to own the problems and forgive.

But then again, having at least a few points of similarities is important because without that, you'll probably just have a breakup over an argument on whether pineapples belong on pizza or not.

- **Pay a unique compliment:**

You might be giving a really honest-to-God compliment to someone, but if it sounds made-up, then it will always be considered made-up. There are certain words like "pretty" and "beautiful" that we have become immune to because they have been used repeatedly.

If you tell someone that they look pretty today, and they actually do, chances are that ten other people said the same to them, especially if they are women. They might say thanks, but honestly, they couldn't care less. They won't even remember you by the end of the day.

But instead of telling them how pretty they are, if you mention how you love the shade of their eyes and how deep they look, now that's something that would make them smile for the whole day. Be specific and personal while paying compliments to people. If you're a guy trying to impress a girl, this is a ninja technique that's going to help you a lot. More on that in **"Chapter 8: Dating Perfection."**

- **Ask for an opinion:**

Now this is something that I touched briefly before as well. Do not be shy to ask for an opinion from people. You do not need to ask them about their views on the current financial situation of the country, but simply asking them about whether they have watched a particular film or tv show can be a great way of generating a great conversation.

- **Focus on the little details:**

Some of us just can't remember people's names (guilty as charged) and that is something that can make others feel really unimportant. While you're talking to someone for the first time, try remembering their name, face and any other details that they pinch in like how their mom acts with them or their children's names. The next time you talk to them, if you bring up such minute details of information, they would feel important as you remembered what they had told you about themselves.

When people tell you details about themselves such as their name, they are giving you access to registering themselves as an individual in your mind. Do not lose that access because you simply weren't paying enough attention. Ever wondered how many promotional emails refer to you with your first name? The reason is that they are playing with basic human psychology. Research suggests that we tend to be more attentive and open with someone when they refer to us with our name.

# The art of keeping the conversation alive

Now that you've understood how the first sparks are ignited, you need to be using them for lighting up the real fire. In this section, we will be focusing on how to continue the conversation in order for keeping it in flow. Some of these points will cover aspects that you need to master, while others will discuss elements that need to be deleted from your conversations. If you work on the following factors, you are definitely going to master the art of conversing with people.

- **Choice of words:**

Believe it or not, your vocabulary can have a huge impact on how people perceive you. Some people can say the cheekiest of things and get away with it while others might even be trying to help someone out, but end up looking like the bad guy instead. The only difference between these two types is in the choice of words in their sentences.

Only if you use positive synonyms of words, people would start feeling positively about you. Let's say you're really late for a meeting and finally reach the conference room where it was supposed to be held. People are already sitting there, waiting for you.

Now you could either say, "Sorry for being so late," or "Thank you for waiting, everyone!" Both have a different feel to them. The first one makes you instantly look like the one at fault, while the second option hails everyone else for being kind enough to wait.

Another example of this would be if a guy goes up to a girl and compliments her by saying, "You look really pretty." while another one says, "Wow, you look gorgeous!" Chances are that the second compliment sticks with her for a longer time.

- **Be present:**

When you're talking to people, then giving them your full attention should be your priority at all times. When you talk to them, be mentally present. Do not use your phone, do not look at how weird the crow looks when it flies, and most certainly, do not think of that sandwich that you had in the morning. Give the other person your complete and honest attention and in return, you'll receive much love and devotion from them as well.

If you want to look at a screen, do that at home. When you're with other people, keep that phone stashed in your pocket or bag and do not look at it until it's necessary. I taught you a few techniques in **"Chapter 3: Body Language"** to look like you're paying solid attention to people that are talking to you. These involve nodding, smiling and periodically repeating a summary of what the other person said. But you do not need to force all of this if you actually are listening.

No need to learn to look like you're paying attention when you, in fact, are paying attention.

- **Don't pontificate:**

I already covered this point in good depth under the sub-heading of "Dogmatism" in the "Sins of speaking" section. But it is worth mentioning that if you wish for your individual opinions to be stated as facts without anyone daring to object you, then you should write a damn blog!

Bill Nye said: "Everyone that you ever meet knows something that you don't."

The secret to success is to always be willing to learn more and more every day from every person. We all have different experiences, hence we all are better at something from someone else. Learn to be calm enough to understand that people have their opinions and that they might not agree with yours. You do not need to be mad at them because of that. Instead, look for opportunities to learn from them and always be ready to change your opinion because of the newly acquired knowledge that you gain from them.

- **Go with the flow:**

Research suggests that the average person speaks at a rate of 225 words per minute, while most of us can understand speech at up to 500 words per minute. Now, you must often have noticed all these weird thoughts popping into your head while people speak to you. Like you're talking to this person and they say something which reminds you of something else, and now all the time while they speak from that point on, you're just thinking about this great topic or question that has struck you, regardless of whether the person you're talking to even answered it while you were zoned out.

The reason for this is that our brain tends to add those 275 words per minute into our mind to use itself to the limit. We are not focused and present in the present, rather we're thinking way ahead of it. And that's not a positive thing to do if you're not a scientist.

Remember to take each topic and question one at a time. Go with the flow and do not try to disrupt it at any point.

- **It's okay to accept that you don't know:**

I mentioned in the introduction to this book that there are certain social kings who have the ability to speak about anything and make you believe in what they have to say. Now, you might think that this point goes as a contradiction to that; you can't talk like you know everything if you accept that you do not know it.

But it is important to understand that in order for you to pull that feat off, you need to have at least some sort of prior information about the subject. If you do not know anything about a subject, it is better to make that clear to the person that you're talking to instead of faking it. This only makes you a bigger person because you're willing to accept that you do not know everything and that you're open to learn about the subject.

- **Don't equate your experience with theirs:**

If someone mentioned that you should tell other people about your sorrows while they talk about theirs to make them feel like they're not alone, then you'd be wise not to take their advice. No matter how much you believe in that, it's never the same for everyone.

Each of us has different factors playing in our individual lives and that's why they can't be compared. If someone's telling you how much their day sucked, don't reply with "MOOD!" or "Same!" Instead, try to ask them about what made it such a bad day and just listen to their story. Don't steal their thunder!

- **The details don't matter:**

This is a very important part of story-telling. Some people have perfected this art while others struggle in captivating their audience while they tell them a life story. The reason is that the latter get stuck in parts that are of no relevance to the people who are listening.

It doesn't matter if it happened on 4:54 or 5:44 as long as it happened! People care about the events, not about when, how and why. So, when you tell them about a life story, leave the unnecessary details out. Because if you don't, they will just hit you with a "Damn, that's crazy, bro!" in the end when in reality, they stopped listening a long time ago.

- **Be brief:**

Have you ever heard of the phrase, "less is more"? Well, that rule applies over here. In basic English grammar, if two correct variations of the same sentence exist, then the one with lesser number of words is chosen as the better option.

Remember that while talking to people, do not keep rephrasing the same stuff over and over again just to make a point. That makes people lose interest and your words lose their value. Be brief and concise and let them talk as well. If you see that the other person isn't interested in what you have to say, just don't say it.

Always think of your words as too precious to be used excessively. Ever heard of that guy, Isaac Newton; the one who discovered gravity? He was elected as a member of the British parliament and it is reported that the only time that he spoke in the parliament during his tenure from 1689-1690 was to give a speech that goes: "The window needs closing." That's one of the smartest people in human history; learn something from him!

- **Learn to listen:**

You might say, "I get all of the other points being mentioned in this section, but how does listening become a part of my speaking skills?" The answer is simple: both go hand in hand. A good listener is always a good speaker. People tend to like those who have the patience to hear them out.

At times, all that we want is for someone to just listen to us while we rant. We don't want their opinion, because we tend to relate opinions to judgments. We just want them to listen to us and by the time we are done, we want the matter never to be discussed again.

Listening and staying quiet is important, but it is also important to listen, reflect and then speak on the matter. If you're going into each conversation without having the patience to listen, you are never going to learn anything from it. You will always leave with the same amount of knowledge because you weren't open towards the knowledge that was being poured down at you.

Buddha said, "If your mouth is open, you're not learning."

At times, excessive speaking gets us into a lot of trouble. There are certain situations where you only need to listen and act upon what is being told to you. A great example of this is explained by Calvin Coolidge, who says: "No man ever listened his way out of a job."

If you're just listening and making sure that you comply with the instructions given by your boss, you probably have a better chance at becoming "employee of the month" rather than being kicked out of your job.

## Avoiding arguments: how not to offend anyone with your words

In the modern day and age, any conversation can quickly turn into a disastrous argument. The reason is that everybody's just so emotionally attached with their standpoints that they can not bear people disagreeing with them. This is partly due to the social media revolution that we are currently experiencing because we have become far more inexperienced at socializing without a screen between us and the world.

All of us interact with most people through a screen. That means that people are bolder in projecting their views because they know that no one can directly harm them through their phone or computer. Bolder and controversial articles or posts tend to get more ratings; both from people that agree and disagree.

Expressing through a screen has also increased problems with people reading each other's vocal expressions and body language. Often you would find people fighting over the fact that one of them just "sounded rude." That either means that the person who said it does not know how to use their words and tone effectively, or the one who heard them does not know how to better register these words and tones.

Pew Research conducted a study on 10,000 American adults and found that today we are more polarized and prone to arguing over our firm beliefs as we were ever in human history. This means that we are less likely to compromise over our faiths now than ever.

Arguments occur mostly because we are not willing to listen to others. You might have experienced this many a time on talk shows or in real life that both people are just bombarding each other with their noise, not willing to listen to anything that the other person has to say.

Below, I will be enlisting some important points to consider for avoiding arguments in your social circles. Understand and implement them in life, and you'll be living a far easier and socially acceptable life.

- **Learn to ignore:**

I realized this strength in my character a couple of years ago. And it was slightly queer to think that this trait could actually be a strength for me. I was living an extremely calm life because I just didn't care about correcting people or making them believe in what I believed.

Understand that it is not your responsibility to correct everyone, neither is it upon you to propagate something really important in the world. You might be doing something great for the world, but whenever you're willing to tell people that they are wrong, you will receive hostile reactions in return. Now, correcting the world might be a very noble thing to do, but the reality remains that it will come at a cost and that cost is your social integrity.

To live an easier life, you shouldn't be caring whether someone is racist or not a feminist or is a feminist or they belong to a different religion. Let me ask you this: how many times have you seen people agree to their being wrong all their life? (Excluding films and fictional novels, of course.) The answer is probably never. People in this day and age consider agreeing to their being wrong as a sin and as a form of self-depreciation.

Your arguing with them and telling that they are wrong about something is probably only making you waste useful energy, precious words and social integrity that is very hard to regain. Because believe it or not, people who disagree with you, probably dislike you as well.

Now, unless the other person is doing or saying something extremely inhumane, like advertising pedophilia, domestic abuse, slavery, or something else of the sort, you should just internally think how sick they are and move on. Now this might come under the category of being a "snake", but at least you're a smart one with a better social life!

- **Compromise:**

This is a very important factor not just in social life, but also in business. You can never have it all exactly the way you want. This is how life and negotiations roll. You will have to ensure that some of what you want is agreed to, but not push it till an extent that you're not willing to compromise on anything that the other person wants. Let's say you want one thing while your business partner wants the other, now if you completely disregard them and keep doing what you like, your company or business is destined to destruction. In life, you will always have to make compromises.

Relationships are another great example of this. If only one person keeps compromising in the name of love and sacrificing their choices so you can have everything that you want, soon there will come a time when they are sick and tired of it and that's when all of it ends.

Learn to agree with others as well and find middle-grounds for such situations. That is another secret for leading a less controversial life.

- **Learn how to disagree with people:**

The best disagree-ers (wow, I'm rocking this vocabulary thing, aren't I?) are those who stay calm, collected and cool. They never let anything get to their nerves and certainly never look like they were taken off-guard with a statement.

A great technique to use while disagreeing with someone is to say: "Yeah, you might be right. But isn't it also a fact that..." and then continue with what your actual opinion is. You do not actually believe that the other person is right, but just letting them know that you agree with at least some of what they say will give them the feeling of you having compromised your beliefs for them. This would in turn increase your chances of their changing their own stance for you.

This works exactly on the mechanism of business deals, as described above. If you compromise, the other person is more willing to do the same. You can't expect them to feel like they are completely wrong while you are completely factual in everything that you say.

Also, keep your aura calm and composed. The minute you start showing wrath and effects of losing your cool, that's when all your chances of winning the argument go down the hill. Listen to others so you can create points to refute in your head. While you're disagreeing, back them up with a good amount of facts rather than opinions. Just telling that you "heard" something doesn't sound a solid enough rebuttal.

## Becoming a part of group conversations

Are you someone who's constantly ignored in that Whatsapp group or who's problems or absence is ignored by fellow group members in real life? If that is so, then this part of the chapter will help you redress any such problems that you are facing.

Becoming an important part of a group or group conversations is an art that a few people are able to master naturally. Others, no matter how hard they try, are always side characters; people who are definitely a part of the group, but are never missed during their absence.

If you follow the tips that I'll be outlining below, you will be able to understand the art of becoming a part of group conversations and slowly, as you gain more exposure in the group through visibility in conversations, you will become an integral part of the group itself.

- **Find group leaders:**

Each group has a center of attraction: a person or a couple of people that everyone looks up to. Without these people, the group stops functioning. It's as if they are the main characters in the identity of the group.

Your task is to identify these characters and socialize with them. If you put great effort in socializing with the side-characters of a group and come to great terms with them, you will still remain unnoticed as the people you socialized with are quite unnoticed themselves.
Identify the leaders and talk to them. Channelize your energy towards replying to what they say in the group and once they start replying to what you have to say, then your presence automatically becomes far more obvious to everyone else.

- **Give your say:**

This is an important factor for the shy ones out there. No one has ever become the center of attraction of a group by remaining timid and silent. You need to talk to people confidently and have your say in decision making.

Let's say your group wishes to go out and have lunch. Now, you have the prospect of having your say in where you guys should go and eat. Remaining silent slowly fades you away from the center. If you give your input into this decision, people are noticing that an option has been floated by you and are now considering it. This makes you visible and more important.

- **Find group interests:**

I mentioned this for initiating one-on-one conversations and would be taking this into account for groups as well. You need to find what your group likes. What are their interests, what drives them crazy, what bores them or what hypes them up!

Once you find these topics, you need to bring those topics up that everyone enjoys. People remember who brought something cool up and if they love a topic and can't stop talking about it, this automatically makes you important and visible.

# Chapter 6
# Social Momentum and Calibration

If you are socially awkward, then chances are that you might be feeling overwhelmed with all this information that has been bombarded at you. Thoughts such as the following might have struck your head, "You know, all of this sounds great to me, but I don't think it's something that I can do."

That is partially true. To be honest, I don't expect you to just go out there and change your life; let's leave that for unrealistic romcoms, shall we? But you can definitely reach that point where you feel socially confident and unstoppable by practicing over time. It's not an overnight process, but a process that definitely works, nonetheless.

Till now, I refrained you from going out and socializing with strangers to make new friends. I taught you the basics of body language, tonality and speech and told you to practice on existing friends and family. But now is the time that we step out into the real world.

For this, you will have to create a social momentum. Chances are that up till now, you haven't socialized much with new people or began a valiant effort at socialization. You will have to take all of this, step by step. It's as if the final product that you're striving for is a cross-country marathon and you haven't even jogged for years!

You don't just go out there one day and run all the way to the finishing line. You take months before reaching that point and actually just start one day by going out there and lightly walking. It takes days before you start jogging and weeks before you're finally running.

**Reasons why you might have failed in creating a social momentum:**

There are broadly only two reasons why you might have failed to create social momentum in your life up till this point. These are:

- Procrastination
- Social anxiety

I will be discussing both these points briefly and providing you with valuable techniques to overcome these problems. Remember that they are quite different from each other and require two separate approaches. You might also suffer from both issues simultaneously, so make sure that you read the complete chapter as it is short and contains practical techniques to help you become better at social intelligence.

# Procrastination and its cure!

Are you one of those people who know that they really should be getting on with a certain assignment that has been pending for ages at their desk. Then, once you reach the desk, you realize, "Wow… I have one *dusty* desk!" Then you think to yourself, "I don't like dusty desks. So, I think I need to clean it."

Now you leave the room to go find something to clean your desk with. On your way to find a cloth, you remember how you haven't tagged someone in a meme all day. So, naturally, you take out your phone and start looking for a funny meme. While you're scrolling through Facebook, you find this awesome sale on some online clothing brand, and you know you need clothes to live. So, now you're shopping! Hours pass before you realize that you were actually supposed to do your assignment.

You're not stupid, so you won't just delay it. But 8:37 is such a weird time to start something, right? So, you'll start at 9:00 sharp! Up until the clock strikes 9:00, you're thinking about how great this assignment is going to be and how much your boss or teacher will love it. By the time it's 9:00, you're too tired from all that thinking so you decide you'll just do it tomorrow. If that is you, then you are officially eligible for the Pro-Procrastinator's Club Membership.

Understand that procrastination isn't a problem. Being a procrastinator means that your mind has plenty of capacity to think and be creative, you just need to be able to channelize your creativity and thinking capacity. This all sounds hard, but I will teach you how.

**Tips for beating procrastination so you can get off your back and start socializing:**

Here are a few tried-and-tested techniques for ending procrastination.

- **Positive or negative visualization:**

    This technique refers to thinking about your goal. If you want to become a social person, then think about the benefits of working on your socializing skills and achieving the aim of becoming a social king. This is known as positive visualization. Negative visualization would mean thinking about how bad it could go for you if you continue living like this for the rest of your life.

This works differently for different people. You just need to find what drives you better to do something; the positive thoughts of how great it would be if you do, or the negative thoughts of how bad it is if you don't.

- **Breaking down your task:**

Breaking your task down into smaller chunks can help you complete it effectively. While using this technique, just focus on getting the next chunk of work done. Once you reach one milestone, set out for the next one and just focus on its completion. Small steps can help you achieve a monumental task at hand. Later in this chapter, I will outline small step-by-step tasks for creating a social momentum and I highly advise you to follow them.

- **Just do it:**

For some people, this technique works best. Don't think about how big the task of socialization is or how you need to break it down. It makes many people perceive that the task at hand is impossible. You just need to jump into it. More often than not, you'll find that you were over-estimating the length of this task and that you can actually do it once it starts flowing. Remember I talked about your first words in a conversation being the floodgate? The same logic applies here. If you start, everything else would flow into place.

- **Make up time limits:**

This is useful for people with shorter spans of interest or focus. Set up imaginary time limits in your head for 10 or 15 minutes. Your goal should be to constantly work on the task at hand during that time limit, tricking your mind into urgency. Once a time limit ends, start another one!

- **Reframe tasks:**

Using this technique will help you conquer your psychology to a great extent. Reframing tasks refers to thinking about the task at hand in a more positive manner than you usually would. If you have a task to compliment strangers, try thinking of it like: "Today, I get the chance to make someone's day special by complimenting them." Anything that gets you going!

- **Social accountability:**

If you find that you are almost never able to rewire your brain into making it complete your socialization tasks, then you can ask a friend or someone from your family to check up on you and make sure that you're doing what you're supposed to do. This social accountability technique works wonders for many.

- **Using a planner (or your secret notebook):**

Using a planner can be effective. I mentioned in the start of this book that the written word tends to have a holy aspect to it. If you have your routine tasks in ink, that can help you follow it in a better way. It also helps you to stay organized and realize the importance of the hours that you might have otherwise spent idling. If you think that this works best for you, I advise you to keep writing your tasks in your secret notebook and ticking them off upon completion.

# Destroying social anxiety and calibrating your social settings

The existence of social anxiety is something that has been denied for so long by people who don't have it. But for those who experience this issue, it marks their complete existence in its own colors.

Being socially anxious means that you're under the constant fear of being judged. Before going out with your friends, you spend loads of time thinking whether they would make fun of your outfit. If you've won an award and have to go up on the stage to receive it, you fear how you might fall on stage and become a laughing stock for all that witness it.

It is also marked by a feeling of self-depreciation. You think that you're not good enough and that leads to your confidence being shattered and bruised. Many people also tend to exaggerate their natural flaws like a pimple or their skin tone.

This is a problem that can hinder you all your life and one that actually takes a good amount of time to cure. But this is where social momentum really comes in: you take everything step by step and although it will take some time, but when you look back at it in a couple of months, you'll see how far you've been able to come and how much you've grown as a person.

Here are a few great step-by-step techniques for destroying both procrastination and social anxiety and calibrating your own social momentum for success.

- **The intent to have fun:**

All the strangers that you see every day are new chances for socializing. These people will definitely not remember you tomorrow, or even if they do, chances are that you'll never meet them again!

It shouldn't matter to you what they think about you. Just try to have fun. Do or say stuff that makes you feel good. You could even go up to a girl and say the lamest pick-up line that you could imagine; although she would probably ditch you, but you'll have loads of fun in the process. You shouldn't care about her not liking you since your goal is to actually have fun.

- **The "Hi!" game:**

Now, this is where you actually start your journey against social anxiety. Your goal should be to greet as many strangers as you can in a day. If you manage only one on the first day, try going for three in the next, and then maybe move on to 5. You'll see how the thirst to increase this number slowly makes you immune to the anxiety of greeting a stranger.

- **Ask for the time:**

Once you start feeling comfortable with saying "Hi!" to people, then move on to asking them what time it is. It's a simple question that offends no one, and you'll be surprised by how helpful people are only if you have the confidence to ask. Keep increasing your number in this game as well.

- **Ask for directions:**

This could be to anywhere like the closest Starbucks. By asking for directions, you're now coming closer to actually having conversations with strangers. This will help you alleviate the feeling of being exposed to the world while you speak to it.

- **Compliment 5 people:**

Now that you have started conversing with people, you need to move on to feeling confident about charming them. If you do not feel up to it, keep working on the previous steps until you are absolutely fine with initiating conversations with strangers. Then, set a goal of complimenting five strangers daily about anything at all. It could be about their shoes, clothes, eyes-anything!

Remember that you do not have any obligation to stay behind after you have complimented them. Just keep moving forward to the next person that you'll compliment. People would never mind; instead they'll love it that someone complimented them and would remember you and your comment fondly.

- **Change your lifestyle:**

You need to understand that there is no on-off button to socialization. To become sociable, you need to create a lifestyle that is so. Once you start feeling confident about meeting new people, try going out more with your friends and socializing freely. Wear clothes that make you feel confident and learn to just have fun while doing all of this. Before you know it, all of this would become something natural for you and a part of your own character.

- **Cut off from negative people:**

Social anxiety stems itself from rude and negative people around you that actually said something that you had anxiously been dreading from the society. People who told you how unconfident you are, or how unattractive, or how you can't do something because you're not a particular type. All of these negative elements aren't your friends or well-wishers and you need to delete them from your life. No one should be able to tell you that you can't do something. If someone does, they deserve to be ignored and forgotten in your life.

This does sound harsh, but as long as you don't leave these negative people behind, they will always mock you and pull you down whenever you try something for yourself. So, if you care about becoming social and confident, then cut ties with those who don't want to see you do that or who constantly keep you indoors with themselves to keep company.

Remember to keep this social momentum going. Think about becoming better and better at socialization as there is no better feeling on Earth than the feeling of growing and becoming stronger than before. Use the tips and techniques that I taught you in the chapters on tonality, body language and speech once you're confident with talking to new people and wish to carry conversations to greater lengths. Using each new individual as a laboratory for socialization will help you have some fun in the process.

Be consistent in practicing social momentum and you'll find that momentum over time becomes habit. Before you know it, you'll have transformed yourself into a positive, confident and sociable person that everybody loves.

**Use your secret notebook:**

Make your social momentum tasks objective by writing them down in your secret notebook. Keep a tally of the number of people that you were able to conduct your task upon and focus on increasing that number. This will help you see how much you're growing or help you point out a particular problem that you might be facing.

# Chapter 7
# Networking in Work Environments

This chapter is for those who spend time in offices or other working environments where the need or opportunities to interact with other people present themselves frequently. We would be discussing briefly about whether you should socialize with your coworkers, and if you should, then how much of it is necessary.

## "Do I really have to?"

Socializing at the workplace is very important for everyone. The reason is that if you belong to the regular working class, then you're spending majority of your awake-time in the office.

You spend 8 hours a day, 40 hours a week, and 2000 hours every year in the office! It is inevitable that you will have to socialize and establish relationships with people at your workplace. Without that, you're probably going to have a miserable life.

"Socializing with your coworkers is essential for your career," says Alexander Kjerulf. Some reasons why you should consider this advice are:

- **So that you don't die of boredom:**

You need other people around you so you can talk to them and alleviate the stress, tiredness or anxiety from within yourself. If you're always glued to your desk, it will not only get you bored, but you'll also end up becoming grumpy and establishing yourself as the "weird guy who never talks to others at the office."

- **Increased productivity:**

Socializing at the workplace helps create a harmonic environment that ends all kinds of envy and negative competitiveness. This allows everyone at the office to become a unit and a team working for a similar cause. In such an office, employees would still want to be the best or become highlighted, as is evident from human nature, but not at the expense of other co-workers.

Similarly, as an individual, an increased productivity for the group means an increased productivity for you. Knowing that you're not in a hostile environment will help you work better and give the best output that you can.

- **It highlights your presence:**

Being social in the workplace makes people and hence your higher-ups realize your presence. They see you more often and hence remember you among the many other employees that work for them. This can help you not only get into the good books of your fellow employees, but also of your employers.

In the long-run, this might make the difference between you getting a promotion or being denied that right despite working quite hard at your job.

# "So, how much should I socialize at work?"

Now this is a really important question. Always remember that the people at your workplace aren't your real-life friends. They might act like it, but in fact they are just fellow employees who want someone to talk to so that they don't go crazy, just like you do. It's not that they aren't nice people, but whenever jobs and money come into play, true friendship goes out of the window!

If your work buddies talk to you at the office quite openly, chances are that they won't after hours. You do not need to have emotional attachments with your fellow co-workers. Now, you might have some great friends at work too with whom you're always hanging out, but exceptions are always there.

Here are a few points that you should always keep in mind while socializing at your work place.

- **Know the line:**

Knowing the line and making it obvious for everyone is important. You do not wish to do or say something that would make you the talk around office. Establish your boundaries yourself and do not let others or yourself go beyond them.

Again, understand the difference between a friend outside the office and inside. Often, you can crack certain jokes with your outside friends, but office friends might find those jokes highly displeasing.

- **Romance and humor:**

Romance or inappropriate/controversial humor at the workplace is a big no for anyone who wishes to stick long at his job. If you wish to tell a very cheeky or racist joke, then your office is not the place to do so. You do not want people to think of you as a pervert so acting like one is not a smart choice to make.

Gossip travels real fast, so even if you do manage to hide your office love story for long, it is only a matter of time before everyone at the office would know. And that would make for one awkward tenure at the office for the both of you even if you break up.

- **Keep your privacy intact:**

Do not indulge into all the private matters of your life with your co-workers. If they ask you about private topics, just steer the conversation away. Your life outside the office and inside it should never mix together.

You need to have a certain amount of trust in your co-workers before indulging into topics about your family, romanticism, religion, views or sex-life. One day, you might be feeling really comfortable talking to a closed-group of people, and the next day Chinese whisper would make sure that everyone knows everything, only with its intensity increased manifold.

- **Socialize at your best behavior:**

Always socialize with people from the work place when you know you're at your best behavior. We all know what makes us crazy and should avoid interacting with people at such a time.

A good example of this could be of someone who knows that as soon as a couple of drinks kick into their system, they go wild and end up doing embarrassing stuff quite often. If you are that kind of a person, then ditching the night out for some drinks with the staff might be a reasonable thing to do.

Other people might really be emotional and expressive about a sport. Going with your co-workers to watch a sport for which you have an emotional attachment might make you remark something awkward in the heat of the moment. The problem is that those people would probably not understand your emotional attachment to the game and they might just view you as a mentally deranged psychopath.

## "When can I socialize with my co-workers?"

Now, here are a few regular opportunities that most of us get at the work place to socialize. You can use these opportunities to gain exposure in the office which would help you create healthy relationships in your workplace.

- **Office hangouts:** we all know about these, and honestly, as boring as they might seem to you, they are actually quite important for your visibility in the office. You do not want to be that guy that's just staring at everyone while they discuss stories from last night's party because you weren't even present there.

- **Happy hours:** some offices organize happy hours for their employees to have an hour or so of relaxation. This is a golden opportunity for office socialization and should be exploited to the maximum.

- **Coffee breaks:** I mentioned in **"Chapter 5: Conversations"** to cut the small talk and move to something really meaningful while making friends and interacting with them. But this is out-ruled for coffee breaks. Learn how to make small talk during this period. Discussing how the work is seemingly endless is an office favorite at most places.

- **Birthday parties:** some offices celebrate birthday parties for employees or company executives as well as company anniversaries. Try playing major roles in these functions. If you're a person who enjoys planning events or is good at it, this is your chance to become an employee with maximum visibility.

Using all the above tips can really turn your office life around for you in the best manner possible. Also remember to target your socialization at important people in the office as this would yield far better results for you in terms of your career. So, try implementing these tips in your life to see some positive results. Who knows, this might just get you a promotion in the next few months!

# Chapter 8

# Dating Perfection: How to Impress the Opposite Sex Without Looking like a Dunce

The title says it all! This is one topic for which you can find dozens of books and articles on the internet. But I've taken the liberty to go through many of those and find for you the best and most universal tips for perfection in your dating life.

## Dating tips for men

Many men find dating to be a very awkward experience. They are quite often extremely nervous before and during the date and end up doing too much or too little. The secret lies in the balance which, like dating, exists in all spheres of life.

Here are a few very helpful tips for men who wish to up their dating game. Remember to process these in your mind and take the time out to implement them in your life. These are as general and universal as they can possibly be.

- **Confidence:**

Confidence is the most important thing for impressing a woman. It does not only show from your words, but even drips down into your body language; the way you nod, the way you touch or the way you eat!

Understand that you can not fake confidence. It is a feeling that comes from within and radiates into your complete lifestyle. That is exactly why you need to implement the strategies and steps that I explained in **"Chapter 6: Social Momentum and Calibration."** You can not become a pro at dating until you are a pro at talking to and meeting strangers. You will gain confidence only when you have good practice in interacting with the opposite sex.

I can not teach you how to be calm and collected while interacting with women. This is something that would only come through practical implementation. So, go out there and start talking to the women around you.

Also keep in mind the difference between subtle and over-confidence. Do not be confident till the extent that you come off as an arrogant brat. Remain humble and gentle at all costs and never compromise on this fact.

If I would have to choose between being nervous or arrogant, I would definitely vote against the latter as that is exactly what makes you look like a douche bag.

No woman wishes to date a guy that isn't confident in socializing and struggles to look them in the eye. So, as I mentioned, practice makes perfect and that's what you should be doing.

- **Clothing and presentation:**

No, this is not a matter of personal preference and neither is it okay to wear your ripped jeans on a first date. Choose your clothes very cautiously and while picking between two outfits, choose the one that plays it safer.

You might be a guy who can pull off some cheeky outfits, but leave those for later dates (if it comes to that.) Many people have a standard "first date outfit" which might be a good idea if you wish to save yourself from the hassle of choosing your clothes every time you go on a first date.

Wearing a tux is not important, but women can comprehend your choice of clothing to reflect upon how important the date is for you. Try coming off as a gentleman and not a rap God!

Also, one thing that many men (and women) forget, is that taking a bath in your cologne before arriving for a date does not make you particularly attractive or make you smell like a bed of roses. Cut it down to a soft fragrance that doesn't make her nose itch. '

- **Complimenting:**

I have mentioned this to some extent in **"Chapter 5: Conversations"** and would like to explain this a little further at this point. To keep this simple and understandable to you all: the complimenting market for females is extremely saturated.

Quoting a study by Sharon Bolton in the year 1994:

"It was discovered that women received more compliments than men, that women gave more compliments than men, and that women of higher status received more compliments than men of higher status."

This means that your usual, "You look beautiful!" is something that they hear quite more often than you think. Such comments are usually ignored and thought of as fake. So, try being more specific. It can be considered a good idea to compliment a small accessory of hers to make her realize that you notice the little things that she puts effort into.

- **Be the real you:**

Doing a bit of research on someone before your first date is fine. And if you find out that they enjoy music, then it's fine to come up with a few albums that you think they might have enjoyed. But posing as if you're part of a band and know how to play an electric guitar will surely not end up well for you if she wants to hear you play something.

- **Sincere conversations:**

You need to be sincere in your conversations with her. Try not doing all the taking yourself and include her into the conversation as well. Listen to her closely and reply to questions that she asks to show your genuine interest towards what she says.

As mentioned in **"Chapter 5: Conversations"**, skip the small talk, instead talk about something meaningful and deep that will get the conversation straight towards the meaty parts.

- **Make her comfortable:**

It usually takes some time for people to get comfortable with you so give them the liberty of having it. Do not crack jokes about them as this will make them extremely uncomfortable and ruin your date.

Instead, try making subtle jokes about other things in life like work or celebrities; anything that doesn't directly point at them. Another thing to remember is that it is often fine if women make fun of you in good faith, but it doesn't work that way around. If you believe in equality, then you can try. But don't be surprised if you don't go out on the next date with her.

- **Surprise her:**

All women love surprises; it's right there on top of the lists of things that they adore. So, try making some effort into planning something special for them. It doesn't necessarily need to be expensive, even flowers or chocolates might be a good surprise if you're able to pull it off properly.

Such actions make women feel special and can make you achieve that "cutie pie" persona that might take you to great lengths with a girl.

- **Ask for some help from your female friends:**

Exposure to some female friends is highly important in becoming more confident and real around women. You can't expect to better your game by practicing only on your dates. Having such friends around you can help you understand how to act around feminine energy and make you learn as to how they can be charmed.

While planning on a date, take some help from your female friends who would be more than delighted to lend some. The reason is that women love the feeling of being experts at something, and if you give your friends due respect and tell them that you need their help because they are good at something, there is no way that they wouldn't agree to doing so.

When you end up getting a good date, be kind enough to thank them and agree that they really are great at this, because let's face it, you're not losing anything by doing that.

## Dating tips for women:

Although women face lesser problems in the dating field than men do, but there are still some issues that need to be addressed for them. These are a few pointers that can help women come off as the happy and date-worthy girl that every guy wants.

- **Be fun and playful:** the media has made this point a little too important for you, but we'll just have to roll with it. Most guys don't expect women to be deep and philosophical, so you will have to learn to be a fun character. Be up for adventures and genuinely learn to enjoy them. That's the sort of image that makes guys go gaga!

- **Wear what makes you feel confident:** again, confidence is key! So, wear clothes that make you feel good about yourself.

- **Focus on body language:** your body language is actually more important than what you say (can't say that for guys, though.) Guys often are not focusing so much on the choice of words as much as women do, but are more into how you're outwardly presenting yourself. Learn to sit upright, look into their eyes and have a smile on your lips.
- **Don't get drunk:** Self-explanatory and for your own security. Leave this for later if you people actually get into a relationship.

- **Pay half the bill:** please! In this day and age, it is highly unethical not to pay half the bill on a date. You had equal amount of fun, time and food as your date did, so you should pinch in when it comes to paying.

Now, you might come up with a hundred reasons not to ("MEN HAVE HIGHER WAGES FOR THE SAME JOB THAN WE DO!") but honestly, who are we kidding over here? It's not about honor, money, or dignity. It's a basic choice of courtesy on your behalf. Don't just act like you are up for paying the bill but inwardly wish that the guy would pay for the both of you. Take a real stand for this and make sure it happens. No matter what a guy says, he would always appreciate you for having the self-respect to do this.

# 6 Ice-breaking questions for your first date

This list can be really useful to cut the small and awkward talk and move on to meaningful conversations. Choose whichever question you find interesting and write them down in your secret notebook. You can even search a few more questions on the internet to have a wider spectrum of questions for people of all types. This might prove to be of great help for people who find it hard to initiate conversations.

- What's the best meal that you've ever had?
- What was your favorite tv program while growing up?
- Which book or film influenced or impacted you the most?
- What's the most embarrassing thing that ever happened to you?
- Who's your favorite movie star?
- What's your favorite song nowadays?

Not only would these questions help you ignite the first sparks, but would also give you valuable insight as to what sort of person your date is. Once your conversation starts to fall in place with the help of such a question, everything else will just start flowing.

# Chapter 9

# Social Media Leverage for Social Intelligence

We have reached the last chapter of this book and it's been a very dynamic and arduous journey. So far, we have worked on changing our mindset, altered our body language, worked on our tonality, improved our conversations, learned the steps for social momentum, increased office networking and upped our dating game. But the last step is yet to be conquered, and in this age, this step is extremely integral for our social dominance.

In this chapter, we will be talking about social media, its importance and the proper way to use it.

## Importance of social media:

To make this evident for you, I'd like you to consider the following question: How many young people around you do not have a single social media account? I do not know you personally, but I'm willing to bet that the number would barely ever increase from zero. Social media is all around us. It is the new way of living and interacting and we need to embrace it to achieve dominance in social circles.

- **The numbers say it all:**

    Do you know that out of the 8 billion people alive at this moment, 2 billion are on Facebook? This is an extremely overwhelming number, especially considering that the 8 billion people alive include children and old people that are probably not expected to have a social media account anyway. This means that almost everyone who is in his teens or is a young adult currently spends time daily on this platform.

- **First impression:**

Like it or not, your social media account is probably your first impression for most people. Let's say you're going on a date with someone. Do you think they wouldn't have stalked you on your Facebook or Instagram? People would judge you for your posts and your pictures and there is nothing that you can do about that.

- **Insight for your character:**

Your social media posts are actually an insight as to who you are as a person. If your posts are funny, people would think you're a person with a good sense of humor, if they are artistic and meaningful, people would associate those qualities with you. They would hold your social media posts as a better judgment of your character than who you are actually in your real life. This makes social media both a very dangerous yet powerful tool. If you use it right and project positive and likeable stuff about your character, this could potentially make you famous among your peers. The exact opposite could happen if you use it wrong.

Now that we're all clear on the importance of social media in daily life, we have to move on to a notion that many people have, and honestly, it is extremely irritating!

# "Does everything about my life need to be on social media?"

No! Everything that you do, every place that you go to, every dish that you eat, all of it does not need to be on your social media account. This reason is why I personally despise the new trend of daily "stories" that almost all social media apps and websites have adopted.

Yes, you need to be active on social media to be visible to the people around you, but honestly, no one cares if you ate from some amazing place until and unless you're willing to tag them along. You're not a celebrity, so stop acting like one!

I know daily stories are now an important part of platforms like Snapchat, Instagram, Facebook and even Whatsapp, but a story once a while is fine. Do not be one of those people whose story is immediately skipped while people are going through their daily ritual of story-viewing.

Your personal life is also one thing that should remain "personal." You do not need to tell everyone that you're in a relationship because it only makes things worse. The more power you are giving to people by letting them in on everything, the more gossip you'll receive. Now this all sounds really fun when you're the talk around town and everybody thinks that your couple is the cutest, but once things start going downhill, these are the same people who just want new spicy gossip about your life.

Only post what you're comfortable showing to everyone during thick and thin. Remember that you do not have much of a say as to who gets to view your social media content. You might say that you have your account on privacy settings, but what are those settings going to do for you if someone from your friends' or followers' list shows your content to a third party? Only post such content that wouldn't bother you if some unknown person saw it.

## "Alright, so what should I post then?"

Now, to the part that actually matters. How do you screen your content and make sure that your social media accounts contain the most refined and fun content for everyone to enjoy and perceive you as a nice person? Here are a few tips and suggestions that might help.

- **Life achievements:** this is something that should definitely earn a place on your social media accounts. Posting about your life achievements can make the people around you realize your talents and make your presence a lot more visual.

    You do not need to brag about your accolades, though. Always remain humble in mentioning your victories and people would perceive you in a far better way.

- **Funny yet unoffensive content:** everybody is constantly posting funny memes, videos and captions on social media. For those of you that struggle in saying something really funny in a group, this might be your chance of coming off as a humorous one. Looking jocular on social media is far too easy as you don't need to create funny content, it just presents itself to you on your wall or feed. Now the only thing that you need to do is to repost the same thing and everybody will see it with your name.

Always remember not to post anything offensive to a particular community. Racist or xenophobic jokes shouldn't be posted at any cost as it would trigger the people who are on the receiving end of it.

Another important point to remember is that you don't need to post all the funny content that you find. I personally keep a "funny-meter" which calibrates the level of funny for each post. A post could be funny, really funny, this-is-priceless funny or oh-my-God-I'm-rolling-on-the-floor funny. Personally, I like posting anything above the "this-is-priceless funny" point. This has the effect that if someone reads a couple of my posts, they might come to a conclusion that my sense of humour is so on point although what I'm actually doing is just posting selective quality funny content.

- **Meaningful and socially important content:** this is an important thing to consider, specifically for those who just keep posting funny content on social media. You need to mix it up with something meaningful and socially important as well. At times, social situations call for remorse like a massacre or famine. At such a time, you need to post things that relate to such problems to highlight them in front of everyone. I sincerely hope that you do feel partial towards these problems, but even if you don't, continuing to post funny content will just make you look heartless to people. If you still don't feel like posting socially important content, then not posting at all for some time would be a better option.

- **Posts that show who you really are:** do not become completely made-up and fake. Stick to who you are and your roots and post content that reflects your real character. If you're a music enthusiast, share stuff about music that you want people to know or if you enjoy writing, pinch in a couple of literary posts now and then. It is important to actually show the world who you are and not keep them confused or have a misconception about your character. I know many people around me about whom I learned so much only through realizing a pattern in the type of content that they post.

- **Rare posts about hangouts/parties:** I mentioned above that you do not need to post each and every hangout and all the things you eat daily, but doing that once in a while is important to maintain a "fun" character on social media. Now, "once in a while" might mean once a month for some people while once every 3 months for others. But doing this every day would just make you look like a wannabe celebrity and that's not what we're aiming for. It's important to maintain the right balance.

# The 4 big NOs of Social Media posting

These four acts should never be committed while you post on social media. If you do, you'll probably end up looking weird or completely unnoticeable to others.

- **Racist/offensive posting:** social media is a very public place and you do not wish for people to be offended by anything that you write or post. There is no reason to increase the people that hate you as a person and you should refrain from giving them reason to do so.

- **Extra posting:** this irritates people and makes you look like a douche bag.

- **Never posting:** quite soon, this might make people forget you because you aren't visible to them on their social media accounts.

- **Giving your opinion on everything:** I mentioned this in **"Chapter 5: Conversations"** that it is not your responsibility to rectify everyone's wrong perceptions. I know you believe that they are false, but understand that they believe the same about you. Do not go into hot waters, in fact, stay very far away from them.

These are a few secrets for maintaining a great life on social media, and if you follow them to the core, people will like you a lot more than they probably do right now.

# One Small Favor

Reviews are the lifeblood of any book on Amazon and especially for the independent author. If you would click five stars on your Kindle device or visit this special link at your convenience, that will ensure that I can continue to produce more books. A quick rating or review helps me to support my family and I deeply appreciate it.

Without stars and reviews, you would never have found this book. Please take just thirty seconds of your time to support an independent author by leaving a rating.

Thank you so much!

To visit my author page and leave a review, visit the following link:

https://www.amazon.com/Gerald-Confienza/e/B07BBPQXD5

Sincerely,
Gerald Confienza

# Conclusion

It has been a long road, hasn't it? But have you wondered how much we have actually covered throughout this book? We have potentially gone through each and every aspect of your social life in a revolutionary manner; one that you probably hadn't tried ever before!

Remember that secret notebook which I wanted you to keep? I want you to open that up and read those words that you wrote about yourself on the first day; about how you look and sound to people. That day, you were bold enough to outline the problems that you were facing and vowed to work on them.

Today, on the last chapter of this book, I hope that you have been able to conquer as many of those problems and issues that you had. But if you haven't, this is not a thing to worry about at all! There is a long road that still needs to be treaded and those of you who started working on your character have a whole lifetime to better yourself.

Some people are able to conquer their social anxiety and fears a lot faster than others and it has nothing to do with your individual abilities. Honestly, if you would ask me to put a number on it, I'd say that in order to achieve true Social Intelligence, it might take you more than a couple of months of consciously working on betterment in that matter.

Understand that it's never too late to start acting! I do not expect you to turn your life around within the span of 9 chapters; if it was that easy, everyone would have been able to do it. But in these 9 chapters lies the potential of changing your life once and for all!

Ending this book does not mean ending your journey for a better social life. Keep this book close at hand and review it regularly. Those points that you wrote down along the way, they are what would help you now as you move on. But even if you wrote nothing down, skimming through this book once a while can help you reach the sort of perfection in your social life that you're striving for.

Own your life, own the theatrical performance that you're presenting to the world and make it the best one that they have ever seen. While you do, I'll be sitting there in the audience and smiling at the thought that I was able to contribute my two cents for a revolution, for my contribution is nothing more than that! All that you did and will do for yourself is your own effort and you should be proud of that.

Lastly, for those of you who are still thinking on whether they should start working on their social life or not, I would recommend you to just take that first step. Don't overthink this matter as it will do nothing positive for you. Focus on the steps outlined in **"Chapter 6: Social Momentum and Calibration"** and start moving in the right direction. I know that it won't just happen all of a sudden and it's a long way to go. But remember this whenever you're undertaking a long journey in your life:

> Those who reach their desired destination are the ones
> with the audacity to begin the journey in the first place.

It has been a matter of absolute pleasure for me to introduce you to my secrets of Social Intelligence and I sincerely look forward to your benefitting from them. I wish you best of luck for your journey and hope that you are able to turn your lives around for the better.

A Preview of...

# Find Your Passion:
## The Ultimate No BS Workbook

# Introduction

*Is it real? Is it even possible?*

We've all seen the YouTube videos and occasional Facebook ads with extremely successful people encouraging you to find your passion, monetize it, and live the dream life. Honestly speaking, they make for very inspirational ads… until they try selling us something at the end. Deep inside we all want a life like the one shown in these videos. The great problem is that we don't know where to start. There was never a *How to Find Your Passion 101* class in college! Lack of self-knowledge and clarity of our purpose in life is the great problem of our generation. If you, too, are feeling lost, then let me tell you something:

*I've been there too.*

A few years ago, I was in college studying for a degree I knew I was never going to use. There just had to be a way I could monetize my talents and live the 'laptop lifestyle' everyone was talking about. But, because I didn't know what I wanted and didn't know where to start, any new attempt I made at entrepreneurship was be short-lived. I tried to push myself through willpower alone, but, in the end, I was always back at square one. My self-esteem plummeted. The dream life I fantasized about in my college years was slowly drifting from sight.

I was blessed that during this time I met a friend named Sebastian Harth. More than a friend, he became an early mentor in my life who introduced me to the world of personal development. One of the ideas he reiterates in his mentorships is the importance of finding your passion and purpose through self-discovery. I took heed to his words and started looking for ways to find out more about myself, my passions and how I could live out my purpose.

Four years have passed, and things have changed. When I met Sebastian, I had barely enough money to eat- extreme, I know. But it's the truth. I had started a business that I was injecting all my money into. My diet consisted of fruits and bread; that's how financially broke I was. Today, I am proud to be indefinitely retired from the workforce. I live off passive income, do what I love, and have absolute control of where I take my life from here on out.

Advice is a very cheap commodity that you shouldn't receive from just anyone. To illustrate this, during my seminars I always give the example of the college MBA professor who advises his or her students on how to start a business, when most of them have never started one themselves. How sound can advise derived only from theory be? I, instead, am somebody who is reaping the benefits of having worked insatiably on their passion for the last 4 years. From a place of coherence, I will guide you through a process that I have applied on myself and hundreds of others that will help you find your passion and instruct you into massive action.

In the pages that follow, I have compiled a series of carefully designed questions, prompts, and exercises laid out in workbook format. Completing these will instigate self-knowledge at a visceral level, probably like you've experienced before. I ask that you keep an open mind. Skepticism is ignorance's best friend. Only when we come with an empty cup can we get our cup filled. Answer these questions thoroughly and with no filter, and the workbook will reveal things about you that you didn't know yourself.

# An Integrated System:
# Laying Foundations

Here's a secret of overachievers: they have an *integrated belief system*. What's this system about?

A few years ago, I found myself talking with the leading authority in Neuro-linguistic Programming in the Hispanic world, Edmundo Velasco. I had ended up in one of his seminars through the recommendation of a friend. It was 8 hours of intense sessions and I was gladly receiving way more than my money's worth in information. For those who don't know, Edmundo was a business partner of John Grinder, the co-founder of Neuro-linguistic Programming (a.k.a. NLP), a science predominantly used for success coaching that studies human behavior in relation to neural maps.

Immediately after the seminar, I approached Dr. Velasco for some quick Q&A. The conversation ended with a few answers and the promise that I'd sign up for his NLP course the following week. A great journey into the workings of the human mind had begun.

I had always wanted to know what made great people great. The answer soon came. During one of the coaching sessions, Dr. Velasco began an introduction of Robert Dilt's Neurological Levels of the mind. He said, "success and human achievement is very predictable. You see, extremely successful people have one thing in common: they have a powerful and, more importantly, integrated mindset. They have a set of empowering beliefs and values that are in harmony with their life purpose. There's no room for self-sabotage".

A light bulb flicked inside my head. That's it! That's what I was looking for- a sense of undeviating alignment in what I thought, felt, and did.

I must've studied the material on developing an aligned, integrated mindset over a thousand times. I couldn't get enough.

As I continued my path in personal development and continued learning the workings of the human mind, I came across the same concept explained in diverse ways. Even World-class coach Tony Robbins teaches it in his seminars. I will explain it to you in the way that it was taught to me.

**The Workings of the System**

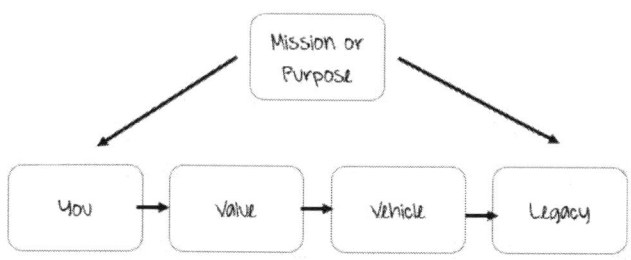

The system above is made up of 5 different parts:
1. Finding your passion begins with finding a mission or purpose that you feel a need to accomplish. Everyone has one. Yes, you do too and if you haven't found it already, we will do so on the following pages.

    *Everyone has something they can't die without having done or contributed towards. E.g. lift people up, especially those who have been emotionally scarred during childhood.*

2. After finding a worthwhile mission or purpose, we must identify who we are. What makes you *you*? As mentioned, we're made up of beliefs and conditioning. The way we define ourselves will play a huge role in the way we're going to take action towards our mission.

   *E.g. If you're a die-hard introvert and your mission is to lift people up, then instead of going in front of crowds of tens of thousands to reach out to your audience, you may prefer to use your writing as a means of communication.*

3. The next step that will help narrow down possibilities even further is taking values into consideration. In order to make sure our emotional and moral needs are met through our actions, values have to be identified. If not, we could be working towards our mission yet still be miserable doing it. What's important to you? What do you value?

   *E.g. If one of your predominant values is leaving your comfort zone, then despite being an introvert, you may still want to practice becoming a better public speaker and developing your own personal speaking style to get your message across. If, on the other hand, you value recognition the least and value sending a powerful message above anything, you may prefer to continue writing but under a pen name. For some people, the use of a pen name is indispensable if they want to bare themselves and their ideas to the world without inhibition.*

4. Finally, we get to the part you've been looking for- the vehicle. The vehicle is the specific action in which you will hone your skill and through which you will accomplish your mission or purpose. The vehicle could be a specific, job, career, business idea, hobby, cause, etc. The vehicle is the means by which you will transmute your desire, your values, your identity, your sense of mission into concrete action that will lead to concrete results.

*E.g. Perhaps it's time to hone your skills in writing. Perhaps it's time to get a job in a large corporation that sells coaching and treatment for those with severe depression. Perhaps you want to open an NGO and blog about your coaching endeavors. You must choose one among the many vehicles available.*

5. There, you've found your passion! You've taken all the elements that make up *you* and transformed them into an action through which you can take your life to its maximum expression. Are we done? Not yet. There's one, tiny, final, yet very crucial step. Legacy. Legacy defines the life of a human being. This brings back memories of me watching the Disney Movie *Coco* with my girlfriend. In this movie, the dead live on in the afterlife as long as they're still remembered for the things they did in life. Once everyone has forgotten who they are, they pass on to the unknown. I thought it was a tremendous analogy- to measure the value of one's life by the legacy they've left behind. Excuse me for going off on a tangent. Anyways, legacy is where we can check if our course of action is really what we want. Ask yourself, "What do you want to be remembered for?"

*E.g. Perhaps for you it would be easier to find a job as a writer with work focused on helping others. However, you want to be remembered as someone more adventurous and entrepreneurial. Then, the logical choice would be to start your own business or NGO and focus on writing content that will add value to the life of thousands, if not millions.*

# Step 1: Find Your Purpose

*Easier said than done?*
I think that's just an idea shared by people too lazy to look and search for information on their own. I don't think it's easy, but it's not hard either. Before we delve into finding your purpose, we'll clarify what purpose is not.

**Your Purpose is Not...**
Something you 'should' be doing. All our lives we've been told what to do and were forced into doing it whether we liked it or not. Remember that boring history class from 4th grade that had you grueling past the coursework the entire year? We've been conditioned to do things we don't want. We've also been conditioned to have decisions made for us. You know, the *go to school, get good grades, go to college, get a job, have kids, retire, and voila!* These are some of the key reasons as to why purpose is so elusive to many of us.

I'm not saying to *not* do any of the things mentioned above. I'm saying that you don't *have* to do them- it's not mandatory. Let me give you a hint: your purpose is never a *'should'* or a *'must'*. It's more of a *'want'*. This *'want'*, when fueled by decision and passion, eventually becomes a personal *'must'*. But, it always starts as a *'want'*. Martin Luther King Jr. was never obligated to fight for equal rights, he deeply wanted to. Actually, he was constantly told by his wife to stop, she knew what could happen if he continued. Despite his fear, Dr. King continued to live on purpose and eventually paid the ultimate price for the freedoms people of all races enjoy in the USA and around the world.

**What Your Purpose Can Be**

During a leadership summit, I heard the speaker say something that has stuck with me until today. "Life is God's gift to you. The way you live your life is your gift back to God". What a beautiful line. There's something I would add, though. It's not just the way you live your life, but the purpose you try to fulfill with it. *If you had to give up all your deeds in life as an offering to God (or to a force beyond yourself) and were evaluated by the positive change your deeds brought forth to creation (animals, people, planet, etc.), what would you want this change to be?*

**What a Purpose-Filled Life Feels Like**
Purpose is not a goal, it's the everyday living. Excuse the esoteric language, but I'm a firm believer that everything that happens to you in life happens for a reason. We've all heard this cliché, however, few of us actually question the events in our life (most just complain about them). *What am I supposed to learn from this? What is this event trying to show me about myself? How can I evolve from this event onwards?* These are the right questions to ask. Why? Because when you take into account your personal story, your childhood, your parents, your personal traumas, the traumas you've seen others overcome, your imperfection, your weaknesses, your strengths, your skills, your talents, your desires, your longings, your role models, etc., then you begin to see a pattern. You begin to see a mission or purpose only someone who has lived your life and experienced everything you've experienced could do.

So, what does purpose feel like? It feels like *alignment*. It feels like congruence. It feels like wholeness. Above all there is certainty- that there's nothing else in the world you could be or should be doing other than *this*.

**In the End, We Make Up Our Own Legend**

Human beings are makers of history because we are makers of stories. Make up a story about yourself until it's one you feel congruent with. Until it's one that sums up everything that is *you*. That is what we will do with the following questions (and throughout the rest of the book). Enjoy the process!

**Questions for Finding Your Purpose**
In the following pages, you will encounter dozens of questions that will help you find your *purpose*. Answer them in detail and write as much as you can. Let your hand move on its own for once.

# Finding Your Purpose:
# 57 Questions, Prompts, and Exercises

1. What would I change about the world, if I knew I could not fail?

2. At the end of my life, what would I most regret not having done?

3. If you knew that you will die 5 years from now, what would you spend your remaining life doing?

4. Describe a life that you would only have in nightmares. Sometimes knowing what we don't want helps us find what we want.

5. Why do I admire my role models?

6. Over the last month, when have you felt most motivated, inspired, and in a state of absolute focus? What were you doing? Who were you being?

7. What makes you happy? Yup, list everything.

8. If I could be granted the power to change the world, what would I do?

To read the rest of this book and see my other titles, please go to:

http://bit.ly/gconfienza

# A Gift for You

Most of the material I write about is centered on developing our inner selves. Thus, as you might've guessed, my readers are usually introverts. I can appreciate that because I'm an introvert myself. However, as an introvert, I'm also aware of our social shortcomings. This is why I have decided to gift you with some amazing material for your growth. By simply clicking the link below, you will have access to the *Introvert Survival Kit* and *Inward Thrive* Email Series for free.

Visit the following site or click here for full access:
http://bit.ly/introvertsk

Or simply scan the following QR Code:

This powerful bundle will help you make massive improvements in your social life. It contains 3 Ebooks and 2 articles:
- EBook 1: Making and Keeping Friends: Developing Friendships that Last a Lifetime in this Fast Paced World!

- EBook 2: How to Stop Worrying and Start Living Effectively In the 21st Century: An Updated Guide to Living Free of Worry in the Knowledge Era
- EBook 3: High Impact Communication: Tips on Getting Your Strongest Message Across in 1 Minute
- Article 1: How to Break the Cycle of Anxiety and Enjoy Social Situations
- Article 2: Be an Introvert and Have an Active Social Life

I also have a special invitation for those appreciate a good read. If you'd like to be part of the review process of many of our upcoming books (and receive free copies!), click here: http://bit.ly/itadvancedreview  I will send you details of what it entails through mail. Thanks!

# Bibliography

- Schwantes, Marcel. "Science Just Figured Out a Way to Help You Instantly Read Another Person's Emotions." *Inc.com*, Inc., 22 June 2017, www.inc.com/marcel-schwantes/science-just-figure-out-a-way-to-help-you-instantly-read-another-persons-emotion.html
- Schwantes, Marcel. "4 Powerful Body Language Habits of Confident People." *Inc.com*, Inc., 8 June 2017, www.inc.com/marcel-schwantes/4-powerful-body-language-habits-of-confident-people.html
- Orloff, Judith. "Three Techniques to Read People." *Psychology Today*, Sussex Publishers, 26 Feb. 2014, www.psychologytoday.com/us/blog/emotional-freedom/201402/three-techniques-read-people
- Moran, Kate. "The Impact of Tone of Voice on Users' Brand Perception (Nielsen Norman Group UX Research)." *Nielsen Norman Group*, 7 Aug. 2016, www.nngroup.com/articles/tone-voice-users/
- TED. *How to Speak so That People Want to Listen*. YouTube, 27 June 2014, www.youtube.com/watch?v=eIho2S0ZahI
- TED. *10 Ways to Have a Better Conversation*. YouTube, 8 Mar. 2016, www.youtube.com/watch?v=R1vskiVDwl4
- Talks, TEDx. *7 Ways to Make a Conversation With Anyone*. YouTube, 11 Jan. 2016, www.youtube.com/watch?v=F4Zu5ZZAG7I
- Riggio, Ronald E. "What Is Social Intelligence? Why Does It Matter?" *Psychology Today*, Sussex Publishers, 1 July 2014, www.psychologytoday.com/us/blog/cutting-edge-leadership/201407/what-is-social-intelligence-why-does-it-matter
- Chen, Angela. "A Psychologist Explains How to Beat Social Anxiety." *The Verge*, The Verge, 21 Mar. 2018,

www.theverge.com/2018/3/21/17147750/social-anxiety-psychology-how-to-be-yourself-ellen-hendriksen-interview
- Ratalyst, director. *How To Stop Procrastinating* . *How To Stop Procrastinating* , YouTube, 7 Mar. 2016, www.youtube.com/watch?v=2zswdWwLG3Q
- Tartakovsky, Margarita. "6 Ways to Overcome Social Anxiety." *Psych Central*, 23 Feb. 2018, www.psychcentral.com/lib/6-ways-to-overcome-social-anxiety/
- Smith, Jacquelyn. "How Much Coworker Socializing Is Good for Your Career?" *Forbes*, Forbes Magazine, 25 Sept. 2013, www.forbes.com/sites/jacquelynsmith/2013/09/24/how-much-coworker-socializing-is-good-for-your-career/#58a0f3fb51a0
- "How to Date Girls." Edited by Wiki How, *WikiHow*, 20 Sept. 2018, www.wikihow.com/Date-Girls.
- Welby, Octavia. "Top Dating Tips for Men (by a Woman) | The Soulmates Blog." *The Guardian*, Guardian News and Media, 6 Jan. 2014, soulmates.theguardian.com/blog/advice/top-dating-tips-for-men-by-a-woman#.W_z2f-gzbIV
- Team, Soulmates. "Questions to Ask On A First Date | The Soulmates Blog." *The Guardian*, Guardian News and Media, 31 Jan. 2014, soulmates.theguardian.com/blog/dating-locations/dating/q-is-for-questions-to-ask-on-a-first-date#.W_z6xegzbIV.
- Bolton, Sharon. *Influence of Gender on Compliment Exchange in American English*. Georgetown University, 1994, pp. 1–1, *Influence of Gender on Compliment Exchange in American English*.

Printed in Great Britain
by Amazon